FIELDS ON THE HOOF

Nexus of Tibetan Nomadic Pastoralism

FIELDS ON THE HOOF
Nexus of Tibetan Nomadic Pastoralism

By

ROBERT B. EKVALL

WAVELAND
PRESS, INC.
Prospect Heights, Illinois

Lobsang Tenzing, the Tibetan artist who drew the sketches used in this book, is a refugee from central Tibet who now lives in India and supplements his income by doing illustrations and pictures. The sketches were made to order to illustrate different aspects of nomadic pastoralism. Scenes were detailed or described to him, but no suggestions were made as to how he should represent those scenes.

For information about this book, write or call:

Waveland Press, Inc.
P.O. Box 400
Prospect Heights, Illinois 60070
(312) 634-0081

Foreword

About the Author

Robert B. Ekvall brings to his writing a most varied background. Born of missionary parents in Minchow, Kansu, China, he himself became a missionary, first in China as a teacher and school administrator, and then in Tibet, as an explorer, ethnographer, and missionary, intermittently, but for long intervals, throughout the 1930s. From 1941–1943 he was interned in Indochina, then entered military service in 1944 as a captain, experienced combat in Burma, was hospitalized with wounds for nine months, and served as a staff officer with the Marshall Mission in Peking and elsewhere in China. He left the army in 1951 as a major, was retained by the Committee for Free Asia to meet and help the brother (Norbu) of the Dalai Lama. He then became a research associate in anthropology at the University of Chicago. He was again called back to active duty in the service, now as a lieutenant colonel, to serve as interpreter in truce negotiations in Korea, as Chief of the Language Division, Military Armistice Commission, and in various other capacities, including observer and interpreter for the Asian Conference at Geneva. In 1958 he left the army and became a research fellow and the chairman of the Inner Asia Research Project, University of Washington, Seattle. He is now honorary curator of Asian ethnology at the Thomas Burke Memorial Washington State Museum, University of Washington. He has published ten books on Tibet and China, six of them on Tibet, and twenty-one articles. He has several major publications in press or in various stages of completion at the present time.

He says this of himself as an author of this case study:

> From the time when, as a lonely white child amongst my Chinese playmates, I was learning to interpret what I read and treasured of my own culture to others of another, and vastly dissimilar culture, the role of the interpreter has been mine. It has remained a constant throughout most of my life: in the years I spent as a missionary among the Tibetans; when as an army officer my experience took me from the Burma jungles through China to the conference tables of Panmumjom and Geneva; and now, as one who seeks to interpret Tibet and its subcultures to the Western world before it is too late—for traumatic change has enveloped the land. Anthropological research is a cold dissection of lifeless bits, and an enumeration of artifacts, unless it enters into an inner conceptual world—alien perhaps but a part of our common human heritage—and brings back an interpretation.

About the Book

This is the first of several volumes in the case study series that will describe pastoral nomads. *Fields on the Hoof* is a particularly auspicious case to begin with, for the Tibetan nomads, the "high-pasturage ones," provide a dramatic focus both on certain general characteristics of societies of this type and on those unique to the Tibetan pastoralists.

The *aBrog Pa* are resourceful, hardy, prideful, aggressive, and generous and carry a culture composed in part of patterns developed in agricultural and sedentary communities—in part, of those special to a high-altitude environment, and, in part, of those carried over from an earlier hunting adaptation. They are Buddhists, and as such should not take life, but, as nomadic pastorialists, they must take life in order to live themselves. And their deities are not those of the settled agriculturalists of Tibet alone, for they have as well their special mountain gods, imbedded in a matrix of folk belief that is distinctive to the high-altitude region.

Fields on the Hoof is a study of the complex interdependency of many factors. The determinant influence of the high-altitude environment and its resources is apparent everywhere in the material culture, from the black tent to the manufacture of fuel from cow dung; the environment shapes as well the characteristic features of personality, the social structure, and the allocation of roles. The influence of Buddhism, countering the survival of folk belief in its emphasis, is significant. Those broad aspects of social system, culture, and personality shared by the high-pasturage nomads with other pastoral nomads, and probably reflecting certain broad adaptations to the ecological arrangements of pastoral nomadism, are yet another level of influence. The adaptation of man to animal and animal to man is an added dimension of great importance.

Robert Ekvall has given us a study in this small volume that presents these interrelationships in complex form. He does so objectively, but with the eye and feeling of the sympathetic friend and cultural participant. So the treatment of the *aBrog Pa* by Ekvall gives us the objectified complexities perceived by the ethnographer, but also gives us a vital sense of how life looks to the high-pasturage ones.

GEORGE AND LOUISE SPINDLER

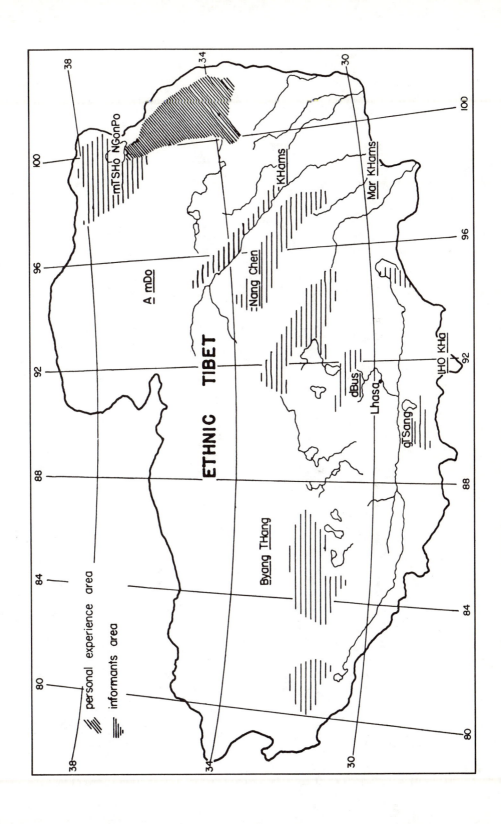

ETHNIC TIBET

A mDo

mTSHo NGonPo

KHams

Mar KHams

Nang Chen

dBus

IHO KHa

Lhasa

gTSang

Byang THang

personal experience area

informants area

Preface

In every book there is something, if only a hint, or the reflection of a mood, of the writer's own life story; but this book is based on many autobiographies—fragmentary, anecdotal, but often with inner depth—of the nomadic pastoralists of northeast ethnic Tibet. For nearly eight years (1926–1927, 1929–1935, and 1939–1941) I had the rewarding experience of associating with these people on a level of such intimacy that they called me—half in jest and half in earnest—one of themselves. I moved with them when they moved, traveled with the grain-trading expeditions, sat in on tribal councils when problems of social control or peace and war were the issues, learned to herd and hunt as they did, and, around campfires and on the trail, I probed for their value systems and beliefs. For their part—unwitting but basic—in the making of this book I owe a debt of gratitude beyond reckoning.

Later (1961–1964) close association with four Tibetans in a research seminar (see "The Tibetan Seminar on Tibetan Society and Culture," *Current Anthropology*, October 1963) gave me the opportunity to check my experiential knowledge (see frontpiece map) and memories with them and thus verify or correct many details as they told of nomadic pastoralism in eastern and central Tibet. More recently, during a year's research among hundreds of Tibetans in Switzerland, I met eight families of nomadic pastoralists from an equal number of widely separated areas (again, see map) and spent many hours comparing what I knew of the culture with what they could tell me. To these two additional sources I also owe much, because the information derived from them has given a much broader base to this book than that of my own personal experience and makes it in some degree an authentic survey of nomadic pastoralism throughout Tibet.

The artificial tense in which this descriptive analysis is written warrants explanation. It is artificial because it is a present tense *as of 1950* and before the Chinese take-over of Tibet. It is a description of a society and a culture, as I knew them and as my informants knew them, that no longer exist as they were, for it is certain that many changes have taken place. In the final chapter, written in a strictly historical tense, an attempt is made to assess the pace and extent of that change and to understand how it relates to survival.

The data were organized over the course of a number of years. During this time I owed much to the following institutions: the Far Eastern and Russian Institute of the University of Washington, for making possible work with the "Tibetan Seminar"; the Wenner-Gren Foundation, for support contributing to the compilation of data and for the stimulation derived from participation in the Borg-Wartenstein Conference on Nomadism in 1964; and the National Science Foundation, for the grant that put me in touch with Tibetan communities in Switzerland.

Also, I am most warmly grateful to the many who have given me personal help and encouragement, particularly, Hellmut Wilhelm, for his guidance and wise advice; Wolfram Eberhard, as he often led my thinking over the issues germain to nomadism; Owen Lattimore, for shared insight into some of the basic problems of central Asian pastoralism; James Downs, who, as he worked with me, gave me assurance that I was on the right track; and Martin Chamberlin, who, by endorsing preparation of a lecture course on nomadism, set me to organizing and clarifying basic data.

In the final throes of writing, I owe much to the efforts of Betsy Frisbie, who, with rare sensitivity to nuance and the set of a phrase, coupled with forthright insistence on clarity, helped me edit and rework the text. I also wish to thank Anna R. Daniels, who, with patience and care, produced a clean typescript from much-mutilated pages.

R.E.

Seattle, Washington
August 1968

Contents

1

Location and Characteristics
of the Area

TIBET IS THE NAME the Western world has given to that high plateau which lies between 78–103 degrees east longitude and 27–39 degrees north latitude, thus placed north of the subcontinent of India and south of the deserts and mountains of central Asia. To the people who live there, it is known as the country of *Bod*.[1] They frequently characterize it as "the Region of the Glacier-Snow Mountains," for on three sides it is rimmed by the snow giants of the Himalayas, the Karakorum, and the Kunlun, and is cross-ribbed from east to west by ranges which are forever white. Even where it tilts eastward toward China, drained by the great rivers of east and Southeast Asia, the valley bottoms are high as mountain peaks—10,000 feet and over—or the landscape is carved into deep, rock-walled trenches as those rivers cut into the Tibetan plateau.

In such a land, wide though it is, with seeming room for all, fields are hard-won and poor. Beds of rich loams or loess are seldom to be found; when discovered they are shallow pockets mixed with rotted rock and glacial drift. Those who work them call them "soil fields." The crops they bear are threatened by drought, hail, and sudden frosts, and with niggard soil and hostile winds, a tenfold yield of barley is a bumper crop. Soil fields are valuable, and, though rocky and with stubborn soil, those who work them are also stubborn, so most of the people of "the Region of the Glacier-Snow Mountains" continue to work the fields handed down from earlier 's, when men first planted and harvesting began.

When pressed by population growth or soil fatigue, the people accept, from

---

[1] Tibetan terms in the text are not transcribed phonetically—the material was collected in too many dialects—but the Tibetan spelling of those terms is transliterated by using letters, or combinations of letters, of the Latin alphabet to represent letters of the Tibetan alphabet. One innovation has been introduced. Because the Tibetan system of spelling employs numerous prefixes, resulting in complicated initial-consonant clusters, the phonetically effective consonant of the cluster—the one which is fully pronounced—is shown here in capital letters. Occasionally, two and even three letters of the Latin alphabet are required to represent one letter of the Tibetan alphabet.

1

time to time, the risk which accompanies opening up virgin land and breaking soil into new fields. It is well-known that the *Sa bDag*[2] (soil lords) jealously resent any violation of their domain.

For the farmers of the land—self-styled *Yul Ba* (country ones) or *Rong Pa* (deep-valley ones)—the soil fields are the basis of their subsistence economy. Working them is the prime occupation, and the sum of all the skills and activities required constitutes the subsistence technique of a farmer's way of life. Within that way of life, the annual yield—scanty and often threatened with destruction—meets subsistence needs. It is soil fields and their care which mark the culture and society of the agricultural subsociety of Tibet.

Many dwellers of the Tibetan plateau, however, develop and tend other fields, not of the soil but better adapted to the harsh ecology of that bleak land. As characterized on the title page, these are "fields on the hoof": livestock, which are the ample base of a vastly different economy. Because it rests on the successful exploitation of large areas of the plateau, the resources of which had been hitherto untapped, and for other reasons, which will be explained later, this economy is a flourishing one.

In form and substance, livestock "fields" and soil fields are far apart, with little resemblance. Yet in essential being, and functionally, within the production cycle of a subsistence economy, fields on the hoof occupy the place in nomadic pastoralism that soil fields occupy in sedentary agriculture. Livestock can be driven to the upland pastures, where they replace soil fields, left behind in the move, and the sum of all the varied skills and activities required for their care constitutes the subsistence technique of the herdsman's way of life. Such fields and the annual yield they produce are often threatened with destruction. Yet if saved, they are ample and provide primitive affluence—a living which is something more than the supply of bare subsistence needs.

These substituted fields relate to the soil in a new and deeply significant manner. It is no longer the quality of the soil that matters. It is the natural covering of the earth—*rTSwa KHa* (grass part), or pasturage, like a green carpet—which is of concern and which supports the herds. No wounding of the soil is involved; but only unoffending natural utilization to sustain the mobile livestock, which move according to the rhythm of the seasons to crop the grass at its best and, by their droppings, give back to the soil compensating enrichment. It is the care of these livestock which makes nearly half of the Tibetan people *pastoralists*; and because what they own, tend, and harvest is on the hoof in wide pastures that require much movement, they are also *nomadic*.

Fields, alive and moving, and the care they require, thus shape a pattern of living and mark the culture of the Tibetan nomadic pastoralist subsociety, the members of which have a special sense of identification with the *aBrog* (high pasturage), where cultivation can never take place.

The analogy thus postulated, in which livestock function as fields in the pastoral economy as soil fields function in the agricultural economy, quite obviously

---

[2] *Sa bDag* (soil lords) are the indigenous gods or spirits of the soil who are believed to have proprietory rights to the land, and if angered can send misfortune and disease on those who have incurred their displeasure.

is not consistent in every detail. Certain aspects of nonequivalency do not, however, contradict its validity. A concise statement comparing the production formulas of the two economies makes this reasonably clear.

The production formula for the agricultural economy is a simple one: (a) labor plus (b) soil, worked into fields and sown, yield harvest and subsistence for the farmer. The formula for the pastoral economy is a more complicated one: (a) labor plus (b) fields (livestock replenished by natural increase), plus (c) pasturage (the natural cover of undisturbed, unworked soil) yield harvest and subsistence for the herdsman.

It is within the framework of this analogy that the life of the nomadic pastoralists—self-styled *aBrog Pa* (high-pasturage ones)—of Tibet will be described and analyzed. The parallelisms which the analogy evokes bring into sharp relief many significant details, and where there are discrepancies they stimulate more careful re-examination of data.

┌─────┐
│ 2 │
└─────┘

The Ecology of an Altitude Zone

ECOLOGY DOMINATES the existence of the nomadic pastoralists of Tibet and prescribes their manner of living to a degree which is only surpassed in the case of those who, like the bushmen and Eskimo, have learned to survive in an extremely unfavorable environment. From topography and climate, two fundamental aspects of the Tibetan plateau, all secondary ecological influences derive. Topography is wholly causal, unless we take into account the comparatively recent geologic upheavals, which lifted the Tibetan plateau to heights which gave rise to its sobriquet "roof of the world." Climate, however, results from topography, the characteristics of continental land mass, and hemispheric wind patterns. It is also causal: it gives livestock distinctive characteristics and, conditioning their care and the yield they produce, it sets patterns of diurnal and seasonal routines; it determines the material used, and styles of, shelter and clothing; it influences the manner in which fires are built, hearths are made, and food is cooked; and, with subtle physiological and psychological pressures, it pushes the development of personality traits which, in their sum, constitute modal personality, providing focus for the very ethos of a culture.

Among all these cause-result factors of ecology, it is at the primary level of topography that the nomadic pastoralism of the Tibetan plateau begins to take on its own unique identity and is differentiated from the classic examples of nomadic pastoralism, such as Mongolian, Turkic, Iranic, and Arabic, which extend across Asia and Africa.

The latter are the nomadic pastoral societies of the "arid zone," so characterized and described in much of the literature [for example, Krader (1959)]. The ecological factor which made, and keeps, these societies pastoral is scarcity of water. This varies from minimal yearly rainfall or extreme fluctuations over a period of years, which create true desert conditions, to moderately scanty rainfall sufficient to provide good grazing on lands which are marginal for the growing of drought-resistant crops.

True desert conditions characterize extensive areas in central Asia, Arabia,

4

and North Africa which, at their best, produce little more than thorn sandy-desert scrub and the vegetation of salt marshes eaten only by camels. Much of Mongolia, Iran, Turkestan, and sub-Saharan Africa is a kind of steppe, which provides good grazing, yet also tempts land-hungry farmers into risky ill-advised marginal agriculture which produces poor or fluctuating crops and causes serious damage to the land. This latter development frequently is the cause of intense competition and bitter antagonism between farmers and herdsmen.

The prime ecological factor which, with only minor exceptions, sets apart the Tibetan pastoralists from those in the arid zone, is one of altitude. Contours of topography and not rainfall-map contours set apart the areas which can be sown and those which cannot be sown. The former belong to the farmers and the latter to the herders.

Altitude as a factor affecting seasonal movement is found in many pastoral economies. Numerous arid-zone nomadic pastoralists, such as Mongolians, Kazahk, Kirghiz, Iranian, and Saharan, move into higher country during the dry summer season. It is in the massifs which rise out of the arid steppe or desert that sources of water and, consequently, forage are most abundant. Transhumance patterns which exist in other semipastoral societies, in Norway or the Alpine massif of Europe, for example, also stem from altitude. It is, however, almost uniquely in Tibet that altitude is the prime factor, separating grazing land from farming land and leading to the emergence of the nomadic pastoralists as a distinctive subsociety. Quite aptly, the nomadic pastoralists may be called "altitude-zone" pastoralists.

This zone—called by all Tibetans *aBrog* (high pasturage)—begins at the upper limits of agriculture, where it is no longer worthwhile to plant oats and turnips, and ends near the uppermost limits of vegetation, in places very close to the snow line, where stunted alpine thistle and scanty "yak grass" are no longer worth much as pasturage. This high pasturage is not consistently contiguous, so mapping it is difficult, but much of the central area of the Tibetan plateau is within it. Elsewhere, wherever topographical contours rise above the limits already mentioned, the land also belongs to the pastoralists in a pattern of wholly or partially isolated altitude islands.

The uppermost limits of agriculture, and lower limits of grassland steppe and mountain meadow, also vary from north to south. Accordingly, the altitude zone occupies different levels of the plateau. At 38 degrees north, the limits of agriculture are 9000 feet, at 32 degrees north, at nearly 12,000 feet, and in the extreme south, at 27 degrees north, at well over 15,000 feet.

From these limits of agriculture upward the altitude range of the *aBrog* varies considerably. It is greater in the north and smaller in the south. At 38 degrees north, the pastoralists live and herd their stock to heights of over 12,000 feet, which gives their altitude range a spread of more than 3000 feet; at 32 degrees north, they go to heights of nearly 15,000 feet, which gives their altitude range a spread of almost 3000 feet; but at 27 degrees north, they take their herds little, if any, beyond the 17,000 foot level, which gives them an altitude-range spread of less than 2000 feet. These figures do not correlate with the actual square-mileage area that is exploited. That depends on the contours of the landscape. Where those contours are steep, 2000 feet in altitude may give only a few square miles of pasturage, and where the contours are gentle—rolling and nearly level steppe—1000 feet in altitude may provide hundreds of square miles of suitable grazing. These figures, based on altitude statistics gathered by me or found in the literature, are only approximations. Local variables such as angle of soil exposure to insolation; degree of protecting shelter from northerly winds; variations in moisture; and the quality and chemical composition of the soil also contribute to local exceptions to the norms thus postulated.

Within this altitude zone of pasturage itself, there are also certain areas of varying extent which, because of other special conditions, are regarded as not suited for animal husbandry. The reedy, insect-infested swamps of the Tsaidam basin are considered poor or useless; the salt marshes and alkaline, yeasty soil of their borders, within the shallow internal-drainage basins of the central plateau, produce little or no fit forage. Some steep valley sides and mountain slopes, because of winds which scour them down to grit, or because they are eroded by violent alternations of rain and drought, are completely bare. Other valleys, in the richest pasturage areas of the Golok tribes, have been stripped of everything green by the depredations of countless mouselike pikas that tunnel the sod, eat the roots, and cause the grass to die, leaving only what the herders call, in grim distaste, "black soil."

Much of the *aBrog*, nevertheless, is an area of ample and varied pasturage. In the bogs—found in parts of the open steppe, many valley heads, and even on top of wide, shallow passes—the coarse marsh grasses are lush and fattening. In favored plains such as those along the upper courses of the great rivers—like *Ma CHu, aBri CHu, Nag CHu*, and *Dza CHu*—tall, thick stands of hay grow to the height of a horse's belly, and where the steppe is drier, or on mountain slopes having a southern exposure, there grows a fine, soft grass which makes excellent forage, particularly for horses. On the shady, northern slopes there is a thicker growth of coarse grass interspersed with flowering plants and shrubbery, which may include varieties of dwarf brushwood. On such slopes cattle graze with particular relish. At the very upper-most limits of the *aBrog*—near slopes of scree, the bare plains of the uninhabited central plateau, or the snow line—where vegetation begins to merge with lichens—there grows what has been called "yak grass": a short, fine grass which lies so close to the ground that only the yak, using their rasplike tongues, can lick it up.

These are the limits and general characteristics of the zone created by the factor of altitude, become *aBrog*, and this is the topographical supporting base of those fields on the hoof which make possible the life and economy of the nomadic pastoralists. Added to this fundamental factor of altitude and its effects on vegetation and climate are other ecological determinants, stemming from climate, which affect the subsistence economy, social structure, and culture—material and otherwise—of those who have been able to exploit the resources of the high plateau. Climate itself is not only a coefficient of altitude but also arises from or is modified by many other conditions: latitude and the resultant angle of insolation, with its daily and seasonal variations; relationship to continental land mass and the consequent severities of continental climate; and air movements, whether hemispheric, seasonal, or as deflected by barrier massifs.

Climate is a complex of many phenomena: temperature variations and extremes; wind directions, velocities, and time tables; precipitation forms, volumes, and seasonal incidence. There are also other less obvious phenomena which derive from altitude: lack of oxygen; intensified ultra-violet ray radiation; and lower barometric pressure, affecting lungs, blood pressure, and the boiling point of water. The climate of the Tibetan plateau, and, more particularly, of the "altitude zone," is characterized by extremes; within those extremes is one of stormy, sudden change.

Where I lived during one year, at 34 degrees north and an elevation of 12,000 feet, the temperatures at 7 A.M. for one-hundred consecutive winter days were never above 0° F and often were as low as —25° F. Such cold freezes solid all bogs, shallow lakes, and smaller streams and during the dark hours holds life in a numbing clutch. Yet, because of the constant and great diurnal range, on a fair day, temperatures in the shade may reach near the freezing point and temperatures in the sunshine—because of the great power of solar radiation at high altitudes—may reach 40–50° F. Within hours, such temperatures thaw areas not in the shade to a depth of up to one-half inch.

Conversely, the burning heat of some sunny, summer days has to be felt to be believed. Excluding certain days in winter or early spring when continuous storm and blizzard may keep temperatures to or below —20° F throughout both day and night, the average diurnal temperature range is between 40 and 60° F throughout the year. In exceptional circumstances, an extreme variation of 100° F has been reported.

One day's experience early in July near the upper knee of the Yellow River, at about 12,500 feet altitude, 34 degrees north, is a good illustration of the diurnal change in temperatures. During our noon halt we ate in burning heat— heat waves danced across the plain—and although it probably was less than 80° F in the shade, it certainly was much over 100° F in the sun. Shortly after we started to travel in the early afternoon, the sky clouded over and a violent thunderstorm swept across our route. Rain changed to hail, pelting us with such force that it was with difficulty we kept our pack animals on the trail, and, by the time we made camp, it had become a blinding snowstorm. At dawn the next morning, the tent ropes were frozen stiff and over 4 inches of snow lay on the ground. By midforenoon, it had all melted in the bright sunshine and the day promised to be hot.

Plants, humans, and animals must adapt to, or develop compensating physiological mechanisms against, these changes. The vegetation appears to have considerable resistance to frost, for throughout much of that zone there are only twenty or less frost-free days in midsummer. This is offset, however, by much and strong sunshine, which forces germination, pushing growth.

Whether or not the humans who share this ecology have developed physiological reactions affecting control of body heat is not known, but the clothing they wear and the manner in which it is worn is ideally suited to adjustment to heat and cold without cumbersome changes and additions. This clothing will be described later in another context.

Livestock respond to these conditions by having uniformly heavier coats and underfur than their counterparts in less rigorous climates. The two principal animals of the high plateau, yak and sheep, are amply protected against the extremes of cold, and their heavy coats are plucked or shorn at the beginning of the summer.

Precipitation is also marked by extremes. Long periods of the winter are dry, with little or no snowfall, which leaves pasturage areas at great heights open for grazing. This and the intensity of solar radiation make the snow line high. In the northeast, at about 34 degrees north, this line is at 17,000 feet; in the south it is still higher. In the autumn and spring precipitation comes in great snowstorms. Spring storms can decimate the herds, particularly the sheep, already weakened by the hard winter. Throughout the summer torrential downpours turn what were dust bowls into what one traveler called "a sea of mud," in which his transport animals nearly drowned. This is also the time of sudden hailstorms of extreme violence, and hailstones the size of tennis balls and larger are a menace to all life.

Winds of great force multiply the effects of cold, and carry rain, snow, hail, and dust—the latter often the size of fine gravel—almost horizontally at great velocities. Such storms hamper, or deflect, all movement of man or beast, and, although there are no scientifically recorded wind velocities, riders are known to have been blown from their horses.

It is under these ecological influences that the livestock of the pastoralists exist, and the forage upon which they depend—in quantity, quality, and distribution—is a product of, or modified by, such conditions. At the highest levels, even yak, best adapted of all livestock to scarcity of oxygen, move slowly and puff like steam engines with any exertion. The herds are scorched by hot, intense ultraviolet radiation and frosted by subfreezing temperatures within the time span of 24 hours. When midwinter cold has locked solid all bogs, streams, and lakes, the stock, backs to the bitter wind, crunch ice and snow for drink and lick the dust in search of winter-killed hay. Some months later, they are deluged daily with rain, while they precariously skirt quaking bogs to gorge on rank marsh grasses. The ecology which gives them existence—and, by its extremes, threatens that existence—creates all the stresses within which the rhythm of life must go on if fields on the hoof are to survive and yield a harvest.

The setting thus created is not without its own real but austere beauty. In winter, dark storms and brilliant sunshine shuttle across the landscape, alternately shrouding it with gray menace and revealing a pattern of dazzling snow fields, white against slopes all yellow with stands of winter hay. Within such a setting frozen lakes reflect the blue of the sky above, and around the yellow, white, and blue mosaic, the great mountains, far and near, seem ever standing on guard, their peaks and glaciers high against the sky. In summer, storms again drop moving curtains of rain and hail on mountain meadows, green, purple, and russet under the summer sun, and in those broad pastures, flowers of every color and form grow everywhere—even to the scree slopes and snow lines of the mountains themselves. Always, in the thin clear air, the horizons are deceptively near.

3

Livestock as Resource Units

E VERY ECONOMY, from those of simplest bare-subsistence levels to those of the most complex surplus-affluence levels, may be said to have the following components: (a) an ecology which provides the setting and the prerequisites for existence; (b) resources which may be functionally broken down into resource units that can be treated quantitatively and evaluated for quality; (c) exploiters operating in functionally determined exploiter units that also can be counted and analyzed for value, and which set, or at least influence, the pattern of social structure; (d) an assortment of techniques by which resources are exploited; and (e) a relationship having many variables between (a), (b), (c), and (d) wherein the number of the exploiters is controlled.

In economies which are at the prefields stage, the existence and inter-relation of these components are easily recognized.

In the simplest gathering society, ecology provides the prerequisites for the germination, growth, and maturation—including fruition—of vegetation. Resource units are estimated in terms of the kinds and nutritional value of fruits, roots, and seeds. They are measured as to quantity and rated as to availability. Exploiters function in units of individuals, families, and groups. They use the techniques of gathering, reaping, and digging. Their numbers are strictly controlled by these factors.

In a hunting society, the illustration is equally clear, but each step is not equally simplistic. Ecology provides the setting and basic prerequisites for existence, but more than germination, growth, and fruition of vegetation is required. Animal existence not only depends on that vegetation but brings with itself as well the more complicated zoological processes of breeding, birth, and growth and is also characterized by movement and competition. The resource units of the economy consist of the available game, numbered either as individual animals or in social groups—families, herds, and the like—of varying size. The exploiters also function as individuals or as groups, but their role is a demanding one, requiring, on the part of individuals, skill, initiative, and courage, or, on the group as a whole, the

9

complex organization of the cooperative hunting unit. Technology—involving weaponry, snaring, stalking, driving, and the like—is more highly developed and requires the products of a more advanced craftsmanship than that of a simple gathering society. Fashioning a throwing spear, for example, requires greater skill than shaping a digging stick.

In economies based on resource units of fields, whether soil fields or fields on the hoof, relationships and processes become more complicated. Farming does pose more problems than does gathering; herding poses many more problems than hunting. Moreover, in the same way that animal-life involvement in a hunting society places greater demands on the would-be exploiter than is placed on the exploiter in a gathering society, so too animal-life involvement in a herding society—within a framework of continuing care and controlled exploitation— places demands on the would-be exploiter for greater initiative and the exercise of more varied skills than in a farming society. In this sense, at least, a pastoral society may exhibit aspects of cultural superiority.

Bovine Resources

Ecology has already been described and analyzed in some detail. The next step is to describe the resources, broken down into resource units, listing them, tracing their origins, characterizing them as regards adaptability to environment, and determining their value and numbers.

In order of their importance, yak, sheep, common cattle, and horses are the principal resource units of the economy, but according to context, the order is subject to qualification. Yak head the list because of their over-all importance, and they may be thought of as characterizing the culture. Yet sheep—as producers of a particular kind of wool which links the economy with world trade and brings special affluence to the society—might come first. Although nomadic pastoralism based entirely on sheep is now unknown, or of little note, throughout the world, the Chinese ideograph for the Ch'iang, who are believed to have been proto-Tibetans of the northeast, does suggest just such an economy. In the resources-development context, common cattle, moreover, have a significance which could make them more important than sheep.

There is some evidence that the Tibetans possessed domesticated common cattle[1] before the yak, and that such possession suggested, or stimulated, domestication of the latter. Furthermore, the possession of common cattle made possible the development of the extremely valuable yak-common-cattle hybrid. The horse too is of note: although it makes a minor contribution to the economy and is never found in such numbers as characterize the typical horse cultures, it does foster attitudes and value judgments which are a part of horse-culture modal personality.

A few other domesticated animals are associated, in a minor way, with the livelihood of the nomadic pastoralists. In some communities a few goats— generally considered lowland stock more advantageously kept in the "door herds"

---

[1] "Common cattle" and "common cow" are used throughout this book to designate the commonly known variety of the domestic cow as distinguished from zebu and other such breeds. See detailed discussion later in this chapter.

of an agricultural community—are found. They are usually rated of less value than sheep, but in western Tibet, one breed, having particularly fine underfur, produces the valuable fiber known as "cashmere."

In the northeast, where Tibetans are associated with Mongols and the country itself is separated from Mongolia by the narrow, "silk-road"[2] corridor, some of the Tibetan nomadic pastoralists have and breed camels of the long-haired, two-humped variety but do not, as yet, have yak as an important part of their economy; they do keep some common cattle. This is said to be because the soil is alkaline and yak do not thrive on the vegetation which nevertheless, is relished by camels and minimally acceptable to common cattle and the numerous sheep and goats. Camel breeding and care are not, however, a typical aspect of Tibetan nomadic pastoralism.

At lower elevations occasional donkeys may be found, but they are wanderers from the farms and have an insignificant role in the economy, although sporadic breeding of mules does take place. Dogs, kept in relatively small numbers, are not livestock in the resource-unit sense, but play an important role—out of all proportion to their numbers—in social interaction. Their particular cultural significance will be discussed elsewhere.

Without yak it is questionable whether or not nomadic pastoralism in Tibet could exist; certainly, in its present ample viability and extent it could not. Indeed, numerous indications suggest that nomadic pastoralism, as distinguished from the care of livestock in various forms of transhumance in an agricultural community, developed only after domestication of yak by farmers who already had common cattle and "door herds" of goats and sheep.

The large, heavily coated bovine, known as *Bos grunniens*—the grunting ox (or yak)—is native to the high plateau, and though kept in a state of domestication in a few other regions (Mongolia and central Asia, for example), is found in its wild state only in Tibet. This alone makes it reasonably certain that the yak was domesticated in Tibet by Tibetans and, thus, is one of three or four known instances of the domestication of a bovine in the ten-millennia history of man's efforts and experimentation in animal domestication.

Taming of the "fierce, wild yak" of the northern plateau is one of the exploits of a legendary Tibetan king.

Domestication of the yak and its results were of sufficient importance in culture history to bring about a change in terminology. The Tibetan word for the male wild yak is *aBrong*, whereas the word for the male of the domesticated variety is *gYag*. The females of both varieties are called *aBri*, but when particular identification is desired, they are called *aBrong aBri* or *gYag aBri,* as the case may be. Both varieties, nevertheless, are the same in all but size, relationship to man, and the slight changes which result from domestication. They interbreed readily. In some areas, domesticated yak cows frequently are impregnated by wild bulls. The calves which result are much like those sired by domesticated yak bulls, but are said to be larger and more intractable.

Wild or domesticated, the yak is well-adapted to an ecology characterized

    [2] The "silk-road" corridor is that part of China which, lying between Tibet and Mongolia, leads to central Asia and through which the silk caravans of the Middle Ages and earlier took Chinese silk to the West.

by extremes of cold and storm, oxygen-thin air, and scanty herbage. Only the domesticated yak makes possible a maximum exploitation of the high plateau, for it appears impervious to cold, able to lick up "yak grass" and browse on high altitude shrubbery, and capable of sustained exertion at altitudes of up to 20,000 feet. At those altitudes, with its great lungs inhaling and exhaling in puffs like the blowing of a locomotive, it can carry a pack or a rider at a steady and, at times, surprisingly fast pace.

Yak[3] handle themselves with goatlike, double-jointed agility in very rough country and can plough through snow like swimmers in their element. Snow-blocked passes are opened by the simple expedient of driving a herd of yak back and forth until the trampled snow can be negotiated by other livestock and humans. Yak answer the need for snowplows in a region where no plows are known.

As the essential animals of a particular pastoral economy, yak thrive and breed at altitudes of up to 17,000 feet. Below 10,000 feet they seem to lose vigor and are also said to lose reproductive capability. The domesticated male yak stands up to 5 feet at the shoulder. Prize animals, such as bulls which have been devoted "to the gods" and thus freed of all work, may be even larger. The cows are noticeably smaller, less heavily muscled, and somewhat fragile in appearance. The horns of domesticated yak are long, distinctively curved, with very sharp tips, and relatively slender. There are a few hornless ones, which are much in demand as riding animals. Yak are inclined to panic easily. When driven in a herd, they crowd and jostle in the effort to stay close together; on the trail, when pressed too hard, they frequently react with the passive stubbornness of the camel. Even the bulls are seldom dangerous, though the cows, when they have freshly calved, become uncertain in behavior and are a hazard. The heads of both males and females are relatively long and somewhat concave and are carried much lower than the shoulders, bringing their mouths close to the ground, like American bison. They have extremely fine and heavy undercoats of fur, belly fringes of hair almost touching the ground, and great, bushy tails so that, whether standing or lying, they are well curtained against the cold.

Wild yak are impressively large. Big-game records cite figures such as 6 feet, 10 inches at the shoulder for a prize bull, and the bulls have enormous horns. Among the nomadic tribes which hunt them, milk pails are often made from the base cross sections. Yak are both wary and fierce, and there are many stories of the ferocity of wounded bulls and their tenacity of life. At altitudes where horses are scant of breath yak can outrun them, which makes hunting on horseback particularly dangerous.

All wild yak, and the great majority of domesticated yak, are black. The instability of coloration which accompanies domestication shows up among the latter. Gray, tawny-golden, light yellow, and piebald yak are fairly common and, with the exception of piebalds, highly prized, particularly if they are matched pairs. In some districts it is considered a bad omen if there is only one animal of unusual color in the herd, but a good omen if there are two or more. Throughout

[3] The Tibetan noun without added syllables does not distinguish singular and plural. Thus, there is little sense is adding "s" to form the plural to loanwords from the Tibetan when there are precedents, such as "deer" and "sheep," in English. Throughout this book, "yak" will be used for both singular and plural.

most of Tibet all-white yak are most uncommon, but in one district near the Koko Nor, a special color strain has been developed and about 40 percent of the animals are white.

The primary importance of the yak in the economy is shown in current language usage. Horses, sheep, and common cattle are enumerated as such, but yak, male and female in one category, are simply labeled *Nor* (wealth). How this wealth is exploited will be discussed later, but the relationship of the yak to *mobility*, in a very special ecology, is of great significance and analogous to the position and function of the camel among desert nomads of Arabia and North Africa.

In those regions, the camel is not only the principal economic base—uniquely adapted to desert conditions—but also the primary transportation factor that makes possible the seasonal displacement of the pastoralist, with his tent and all his possessions, thus making him a nomad. Similarly, in Tibet the yak is not only the principal economic base—uniquely adapted to high-altitude conditions—but also the primary means of transportation, which makes possible: the seasonal displacement of the pastoralist with tent and all belongings; the transportation of his animal-husbandry produce to markets or exchange points; and even the supplementary exploitation of such mineral resources as salt and borax. By this means of transportation, the pastoralist becomes nomadic; his basic mobility paced by the speed and conditioned by the carrying capabilities of the yak. He himself is yak-borne when in very high altitudes, in very rough terrain or in deep snow, and, as a means of saving horseflesh, while carrying out routine chores.

In Tibetan history, there is evidence that both wild and domesticated yak, specified by their respective names, came to have symbolic significance as representing Tibet. The yak is frequently mentioned, with a few other native animals—bear, argali, eagle, and snow lion[4]—as having a relationship with the original mountain gods of the pre-Buddhist pantheon, and reference to a restricted use of yak flesh in sacrifice has totemic overtones. In the religiomythic subjugation of the original gods of Tibet by Padma Sambhava he won his most striking victory over a demon impersonated by a great white yak. The legend of the enmity of the yak and the horse also suggests an early yak-based culture.

Linked with the yak, as resource units of a livestock-based way of life, are the yak-and-common-cattle hybrids. The males are called *mDZo*, and the females *mDZo Mo*. They are found in considerable numbers, but in very irregular distribution patterns. In some areas they approach in numbers, and considerably exceed in total value, the yak. In other areas, they are bred mainly to sell. Elsewhere, they are not to be found, either because—as the Tibetans insist—the higher levels of the *aBrog* are too cold for them, or where—as in the *Pu Ma* lake region for example—it is thought that the "mountain gods" dislike cross-breeding as an insulting perversion. This may be linked with the previously mentioned totemic or symbolic significance of the yak.

The hybrids bring higher prices than either yak or common cattle: 50 percent more, and upward, than yak, and at least twice the price of common cattle.

---

[4] As far as is now known, this creature is legendary, but some Tibetans insist that it once existed as a companion beast of prey to the snow leopard.

Like mules, they are an outstanding example of "hybrid vigor" in the first cross. They are superior to both parents in size, conformation, resistance to disease, and in tractability. The females give more milk and are more easily handled than yak cows or common-cattle cows. The oxen carry heavier loads at a faster pace and have greater endurance than either yak oxen or common-cattle oxen, and unlike yak they will follow head to tail on narrow trails, and on open terrain will follow parallel paths without jostling.

Like mules, these bovine hybrids are of two varieties: those which are a result of common-cattle-bull and yak-cow crossbreeding and those which are the result of yak-bull and common-cattle-cow crossbreeding. The latter variety is less common. The two look much alike, but the nomads unfailingly distinguish between them and generally rate the latter slightly inferior, and price them accordingly.

The hybrids are not only larger, but better built and muscled. Their heads are shorter and less concave than those of the yak and, in relation to their shoulders, which are less humped, their heads are carried higher and more on a line. Their horns are shorter and thicker, and the final backward curve, which is such a distinctive feature of the yak-head silhouette, is much less pronounced. Both males and females are less heavily coated than yak, the belly fringes are noticeably shorter and more scanty, and their tails are less bushy. This without doubt is one reason for their lower resistance to cold.

The particular aspect of hybrid fertility-sterility which differentiates them from mules is that the cows, when bred back to either of the parent stocks, are fertile. The males are gelded very early, but it is said that they are sterile even when this has not been done.

Calves dropped by hybrid cows seldom live or are allowed to live. It is widely maintained that when allowed to grow to maturity, they are the most inferior and intractable of all the bovines known to Tibetans. The females of this generation are, nevertheless, fertile, and their offspring—the result of a back-cross with either yak or common-cattle bulls—as the third generation, are of greater value. This continuing but extremely rare hybridization, is, however, always dependent on the males of the parent lines. It is not a stabilization of the mDZo as a distinct breed which is independently self-propagating.

When, how, and why this hybridization began and became an important part of herd management is not certain. It undoubtedly took place after the yak had been domesticated—presumably by farmers who possessed common cattle as an important part of a mixed agricultural-pastoral economy—and it probably followed soon after. Whether in the confusion and possible perversion of breeding habits which accompanies domestication it happened by accident or whether it was the result of calculated experimentation is equally unknown.

It is widely held that hybridization is not quite the proper thing, either because the local gods may become angry and send cattle epidemics, storms, and killing hail or because it is poor long-term herd management. Valuable though the results of the first cross may be, the line of descent ends with the hybrid. Straight yak breeding, however, produces generation after generation, increasing the size of the herds. Whether by design or by accident, this hybridization was an important and successful step in optimum exploitation of the resources of the Tibetan plateau by adaptation to its particular topography and ecology.

The common-cattle bovine is essentially a lowland animal which appears stunted by the rigors of the climate and is known as the farmer's beast of all work. In the climate of the plateau it is a poor producer of milk, and in the wheelless culture of Tibet it is, with its small size and low shoulders, a notoriously poor packer with neither speed nor strength and endurance. In value it is the "poor man's animal," possessing neither prestige nor place in legend or mythology. The yak, however, is a high-country animal par excellence, possessing its own unique place in symbolism and legend, but it is at a disadvantage in many respects in the lower country, for it does not stand heat well and it crowds and jostles on narrow trails. A cross between the two produces an animal that flourishes at both high and low levels and is superior as a milk producer. By excellence as a pack animal in varied terrain—open country or deep defiles and narrow valleys—it meets a pressing transportation need throughout all of Tibet. It is significant that cross-breeding for *mDZo* is at its maximum among the so-called seminomads, who originate from agricultural communities. This would seem to indicate that cross-breeding of yak and common cattle—begun by agriculturists—was continued as a successful pastoral adaptation to particular ecological conditions in exploitation of the resources of the Tibetan plateau.

The common cattle of Tibet, found in relatively greater numbers among the sedentary agriculturalists than among the nomadic pastoralists, probably were brought from the east. Wherever found, they appear to be one breed (*Bos primogenius*), identical with, or closely related to, the Chinese variety known throughout China as the *huang niu* (yellow cow). They vary in size according to regional distribution. In that part of Amdo where the Tibetan plateau dips low to merge with the more moderately elevated (5000–7000 feet) plains of northwest China, and where, in a restricted locality, pastoralism is based on camels and the common cattle, the latter attain their maximum size, resembling the large, heavily built "yellow oxen" seen in the Chinese provinces of Shensi and Honan. Elsewhere along the ethnic Sino-Tibetan border they are somewhat smaller, but westward across the Tibetan plateau, as elevations mount, they are increasingly stunted. In far western Tibet, where they are relatively rare, they are "small as donkeys" and quite useless, except for crossbreeding. In eastern Tibet too this often is the sole reason for which they are kept; several families communally keeping one stud bull. Red or brindle are common colors, with an occasional gray or piebald; consequently, hybrids vary in color more than yak do. This variety of *Bos primogenius* is important to Tibetan nomadic pastoralism because of its role in culture development and in herd management. Possession of these bovines by early populations who migrated to the Tibetan plateau in relatively late prehistoric time, or acquirement of them by populations who were basically indigenous and had developed from very early hunting or gathering societies, was a demonstration of the techniques and advantages of domestication. This unquestionably suggested the feasibility of domesticating the autochthonous bovine of the high plateau and stimulated efforts to bring the latter under human control and exploitation. Common cattle, because of minimal adaptation to the ecology, were of little economic value, but as stud animals they made possible the creation of a valuable hybrid and were important in herd management.

Ovine Resources

In Tibet there are two varieties of domesticated sheep. *Yul Lug* (country sheep), or *Rong Lug* (deep-valley sheep), as terminology indicates, is a breed kept by the agriculturalists. *aBrog Lug* (high-pasturage sheep) belong only to the nomadic pastoralists. The former are characterized by medium size, fine fleece of medium length, which covers most of the neck and legs, enlarged, fatty tails, and small horns that curl closely on the head. The great majority are white, but black and occasional gray ones are not uncommon. These characteristics suggest that they are a breed long domesticated and quite distant in time and mutation change from any known wild species.

aBrog Lug are quite different, being large with heavy bodies on long legs. Their fleece, which is lacking on head, neck, and legs, is coarse and, at maximum winter growth, as much as 7 inches in length. Frequently, long, crinkly *hairs* which, except that they are white, resemble the hair of deer or wild sheep, are interspersed throughout the fleece. Occasionally, there are individuals which have a complete coat of such hair instead of wool. The uniformly white *aBrog Lug* sometimes do have flecks of tan showing in the short hair of the head, neck, and legs. Their necks are short, and, as heads are carried in a straight line, level with the shoulders, the ewe-neck effect is lacking. The horns are roughly triangular in cross section, average about a foot in length, and spread sideways from the head, twisted in a loose spiral. When in good condition, these sheep are heavily fleshed, with more muscle than fat, and their long legs give them good trail capabilities. They can carry packs of up to 30 pounds for long distances and, in some areas, are much used for transport. Unlike *Yul Lug*, they have no fatty enlargement of the tail, but only small ruffed triangles covered with short hair.

There is a seeming parallelism between the distribution and possible origins of the common cattle and the yak, on the one hand, and the distribution and possible origins of the sheep of agriculturalists and those of the nomadic pastoralists, on the other. It suggests that the latter, also called *Byang Lug* (north sheep—in the sense of the north-central plateau), by their persisting wild-species traits, by their association with the yak as the base of the pastoral economy, and by the origin implied in their names, is the result of a relatively recent effort in domestication by the Tibetans. This could have been parallel to the domestication of the yak in the process of establishing a high-altitude economy based on livestock native to the plateau.

This suggestion is much more hypothetical than in the case of the yak. Two species of wild sheep, the argali and the burrhel, are found in considerable numbers throughout the plateau, but neither one resembles the *aBrog Lug* as closely as the wild yak resembles the domesticated variety. The burrhel, sometimes called "blue sheep," approximates the *aBrog Lug* in size and has crinkly hair; the horns of the ram turn outward to the side in a half twist. Certainly, the *aBrog Lug* appears different from the commonly known domesticated sheep. Quite aside from everything else, its flesh lacks the distinctive "muttony flavor" of mutton the world over, tasting more like "wild" mutton. I have broiled the meat of both "blue sheep" and *aBrog Lug* at a campfire and could hardly tell them apart.

These bovines and ovines are the principal fields of the pastoralists and the base of their economy. From their combined harvests the herdsmen derive the supply of all their needs. In one particular locality a relatively small number of camels also share this function. Among other animals, horses and dogs make their distinctive contributions to the culture, which will be analyzed in other contexts. Without the bovines, the pastoral subculture could not exist, but without the ovines, that existence would be a niggardly one, if, indeed, it would be viable.

Resources Sufficiency

As basic resource units to which exploiter units are related in a harvest-consumer ratio, their total is not known. In many areas no figures are compiled and in areas where, for tax and levy purposes, such figures are reported, they are —for quite obvious reasons—fraudulent or misleading. In lieu of numerical totals, two ratio postulates are yet valid: (a) The resource units (actual count of livestock), which inevitably are relationed to area and, more particularly, to the grass cover, are less than the support potential of high pasturage available under the conditions imposed by the ecology; (b) the resource units (actual count of livestock) are ample for maintaining the present population in relative (by Asian standards) affluence and offer inducements for increase of population.

In discussion of the problem of *rTSwa KHa* (grass part) with nomads from most pastoral areas of Tibet, and in my own observation, a problem concerning actual scarcity of pasturage seldom, if ever, exists. Rather than being over-grazed, entire areas often are left untouched during alternate seasons or even neglected for several seasons. Also, the herdsmen of Tibet, as discussed previously, are not threatened by land-hungry farmers seeking to exploit marginal lands by finding or reapportioning water resources. The *aBrog* remains forever the land of the herdsmen.

The comparative affluence of the pastoralists is well attested in Tibetan history and folklore; they themselves are boastfully conscious of it; it is an acknowledged factor in the wealth collection policies of the religious establishment and shows up in a significant trade index—the only commodity produced in Tibet in sufficient quantity to have an important place in world trade is the coarse wool which comes from the sheep of the high pasturage.

Though not even approximate livestock totals can be formulated, relative numbers of bovines and ovines can be approximated, although these vary greatly according to region. In parts of northeastern Tibet the ratio of sheep *versus* bovines (mostly yak) varies from fifteen to one to seven to one. Among the Goloks in high, rough country, this ratio is reversed and sheep are less numerous than cattle.

Throughout most regions the ratio varies from four up to eight sheep to one yak. In one district of central Tibet, for tax purposes, six sheep count for one bovine (yak, hybrids, and common cattle averaged out) and in a meat market in west-central Tibet five sheep have the value of one good yak. Further west, and on the central plain, sheep are found in smaller comparative numbers and in some areas, *TSa Ri*, for example, there are none.

For a tent family of four persons to have a viable economy, without the sale of labor to wealthier neighbors, the estimated minimum number of resource units again varies greatly. When the estimate is made by nomadic pastoralists who are relatively wealthy—possessing two- or three-hundred bovines and a thousand sheep or more—the estimate given is quite high, at least a hundred bovines and several hundred sheep. Such an estimate is influenced both by the relative affluence of the one making it and by reference to other, wealthier tent families (I have known such), who possess hundreds of bovines and many thousands of sheep. Conversely, modest estimates, based, presumably, on modest scales of living, indicate that, with good management, a family of four can be independently self-sufficient with as few as forty bovines and a hundred, or even fewer, sheep. I have known families who seemed to get along with only twenty bovines and forty or fifty sheep. It is impossible to make as exact an estimate when dealing with resource units of livestock fields and their yield as when counting and measuring soil fields and estimating their yield. Not only are many more variables involved, but over-shadowing all estimates of livestock yields loom the greater risks of pastoralism. A severe winter, with unusually heavy snowfalls, or the unpredictable but always serious course of hoof-and-mouth disease or rinderpest, may, in a single season, reduce any tent family, poor or wealthy, to beggary. The chances of very large and rapid gains are also ever present. Living thus, between risk and gain as he counts and cares for his fields, the nomadic pastoralist finds it difficult to estimate exactly the number of resource units needed for him to make a living.

┌─────────┐
│   4   │
└─────────┘

The *aBrog Pa* and Cultural Identity

E NTIRE POPULATIONS throughout the world are classified on the basis of what fields they own, how ownership is spread within the society, and what ownership entails in labor and reaping of benefit. Populations owning soil fields, for example, are classified as peasant, but there are also those who own fields on the hoof, and they are classified as pastoral. How ownership is spread within that society—individual, absentee, family, community, or state—affects forms of social structure and the relationships within the society. What ownership entails in husbandry techniques, division of labor, cooperation, and the like, gives to the society its distinctive character and cohesive strength.

The pastoralists of Tibet, made nomadic by convergent factors of ecology, the mobile character of their fields, and other, less easily identifiable social and personality variables, have their own name for themselves, accepted and used by all Tibetans: They are *aBrog Pa*—high pasturage ones. The word *aBrog* designates an ecologically delimited zone, but by usage it has acquired sociological and cultural connotations and is difficult to render into one English word. In earlier publications I used the word "wilderness," which has significant aptness in some connotations, but may be misleading in an ecological context. "High pasture" is a good *description* of the zone of pasturage, found throughout Tibet above the uppermost limits of agriculture and upward to the limits of vegetation, which is called *aBrog*. As an adjective, it classifies people, animals, behavior patterns, value judgments, concepts, and the like. There are "high-pasturage" ones, women, horses, sheep, speech, custom, law, and the like, a differentiation contributing to the definition of a distinctive subculture, conforming to the *aBrog* concept, which marks a people. It also is antithetical to concepts of *Yul* (country), *Rong* (deep valley), and *Grong* (village) used to characterize the sedentary agricultural subculture.

Within the *aBrog Pa* are a number of subcategories: the *sBa Nag* (black tents), an agglomeration of tribes in *A mDo;* the *mGo Log* (rebels), tribes noted for lawlessness and banditry; and the *Byang Pa* (north ones), nomads of the high northern Plain.

The *Sa Ma aBrog*

Linked with, but not within, the *aBrog Pa* are the *Sa Ma aBrog* (neither soil nor high pasturage)—a large segment of pastoralists often labeled "semi-nomads." By many criteria—animal husbandry, use of tents, even mobility, and the like—there seems to be no reason for excluding them from the *aBrog Pa*, but the Tibetans invariably insist on the distinction. As the term *aBrog Pa* is antithetical to *Rong Pa* or *Yul Ba*, so *aBrog CHen* (high-pasturage great) and *aBrog NGo Ma* (high-pasturage the real) are terms used to make clear the intrinsic difference between the *aBrog* and the *Sa Ma aBrog*. The fundamental distinction is based on the origin of the *Sa Ma aBrog* and the continuing functional link they maintain with that origin. In each instance, a *Sa Ma aBrog* economy stems from transhumance practiced by an agricultural community which has a large number of livestock, and—because of topographical contours—is near unexploited pasturage.

Development from an agricultural community into *Sa Ma aBrog* begins with the common practice of sending out each morning the *sGo PHyugs* (door herd) cattle, sheep, or goats to graze on nearby pastures and bringing them back each evening. Particularly during the crop-growing season this can cause trouble, for Tibetan fields are mostly insufficiently, or not at all, fenced. Damage done to crops by herds going to, or returning from, nearby pastures is a constant source of ill feeling within every agricultural community. Nearby pastures are soon over-grazed and competition for them becomes another reason for friction.

The next stage is the establishment of summer cattle camps sufficiently near for daily communication, yet far enough away to prevent strays from getting into the fields and to provide the maximum of grazing. Called *dByar Sa* (summer soil, or place), these camps use tents and huts, have some mobility, but are closely linked with the agricultural community. Daily trips are made to supply the farm with fuel, butter, milk, and cheese. After harvest, these camps are dismantled; the livestock are brought down and are kept in the farms throughout the winter.

When *dByar Sa* camps function year-round, this form of transhumance becomes a typical *Sa Ma aBrog* community and economy, but there are differences in the degree to which a *Sa Ma aBrog* community lengthens—in space and social distance—its link with the agricultural community, thereby moving toward identification with the *aBrog*. Some are merely *dByar Sa* camps maintained on an all-seasons basis, remaining close to the agricultural community and maintaining a daily exchange of visits. Personnel are constantly rotated and no one becomes exclusively *Sa Ma aBrog* in work and skills.

Other *Sa Ma aBrog* camps with economic self-sufficiency are virtually autonomous. They move four or five times a year considerable distances from the agricultural communities of their origin, maintaining only intermittent contact with them. Their membership is not rotated, but consists of fragments, or moities, of families who, on a long-term basis, become exclusively *Sa Ma aBrog*, developing animal-husbandry skills and having nothing more to do with agriculture. Only in origin and in the continuing economic interrelation with it (livestock of the farmers being pastured by their *Sa Ma aBrog* relatives and the relatives, in turn, counting on the farmers for grain) do they differ from the *aBrog CHen*. Even at this advanced stage of change, they are never considered "real nomads," but remain *Sa Ma aBrog*.

The herds of the *Sa Ma aBrog* also differ from the herds of the *aBrog Pa* in their composition. There are fewer yak and sheep and a greater number of common cattle and goats. Some of the donkeys of the base farm are pastured with them, and frequently there are more bovine hybrids. Indeed, many of the *Sa Ma aBrog* specialize in the breeding of these hybrids. Ownership of livestock is also more complicated. Since only a limited number of farm families have sufficient resources (both wealth and manpower) to set up a *Sa Ma aBrog* tenthold, poor farmers are obliged to put whatever livestock should be pastured away from the immediate vicinity in the care of the *Sa Ma aBrog* units of their wealthy neighbors. This is done on a sharecrop basis or by payment in service when extra help is needed. Thus the ownership of the herds, for which a single *Sa Ma aBrog* tenthold is responsible, may be spread among several families of the agricultural community. Caravan managers also prefer to leave sick or worn-out animals for recuperation at the *Sa Ma aBrog* because, being less nomadic, it is more easily located at a later date. Such arrangements give the *Sa Ma aBrog* tenthold a broader economic base than the pastoral branch of a single agricultural family could supply.

Sa Ma aBrog problems of pastoralism, and the techniques and routines in the care of livestock fields are generally similar to those of the *aBrog*. This is particularly true with regard to seeding, an important part of herd management, and harvest, and in the creation of material-culture artifacts. In these and related aspects of the economy, much of what will be said of the *aBrog Pa* also applies, with minor qualification, to the *Sa Ma aBrog*. Essential differences between the two do, however, exist, particularly with regard to social structure and basic mobility. As frequently and easily as they move, the *Sa Ma aBrog* yet remain tied by many links to a fixed base. Communal and individual freedom, which stems from relatively untrammeled mobility, is lacking, and the social and psychological affects which flow from such mobility are also lacking, for the *Sa Ma aBrog* are not completely nomadic—they are, at most, seminomadic.

A function of this halfway stage between sedentary agriculturalism and nomadic pastoralism is of considerable significance, both as to what it represents in *preparation* for change and how it confirms *direction* of change. The *Sa Ma aBrog* institution is an important schooling in the techniques of pastoralism and the routines and habits which accompany it. Having become well-trained, individuals frequently move on and find a place for themselves among communities of the *aBrog*. Sons, or younger brothers, of an agricultural family, charged with the responsibility of the family *Sa Ma aBrog* tenthold and herds, often try to find wives from among the *aBrog*, for those women are skilled in their role within a milking and buttermaking economy. When this happens, the tenthold then moves a long step toward identification with the *aBrog CHen*, and the affinal link may facilitate change-over to full nomadism.

The significance of the *Sa Ma aBrog* as an indication of *direction* of change lies in the fact that invariably it represents movement, or shift of population, *from* sedentary agriculturalism toward nomadic pastoralism, and never the other way around. The trend is not to settle down, but to develop and practice movement from the soil to the high pasturage. The syllable order of the term—first *Sa* (soil) and then *aBrog* (high pasturage) epitomizes the direction of this demographic shift. See Downs (1964:1115–1119) and Downs-Ekvall (1965:169–184) for more details about these seminomads.

People of the *aBrog*

The nomadic pastoralists who own the livestock fields of Tibet are Tibetans. This is not as banal a statement of the obvious as it may seem. Because of the many marked differences in culture and personality between the nomads— variously called Drogpa, Dokpa, and the like—and other Tibetans, it has been suggested that the former are a different race. The fact that in some Tibetan tax records the *Bod Pa* (Tibetan ones) and *aBrog Pa* (high-pasturage ones) are listed separately has led to the contention that the "high-pasturage ones" are later arrivals and racially somewhat different. Until recently, however, the term *Bod Pa* was applied only to the inhabitants of the two central provinces of Tibet, although currently, in the search for a sharper national and ethnic identity, the refugees are applying it to all Tibetans. *Bod KHa Ba* (Tibetan part ones), the historical, broadly inclusive term for all Tibetans, includes the *aBrog Pa*.

The Tibetan people, by the great variety of physique and physiognomy found among them, seem to be an ethnic amalgam of many racial strains. Prince Peter of Denmark and Greece, who had the measurements of five thousand refugees taken as they came into India, told me that those measurements well support the careful observer's impression that there is great diversity among the people.

No comparative measurements have been taken of the nomads, as distinguished from other Tibetans, but they partake, at least, of this general diversity. There are indications that they may have received some additional Turanian and Mongolian admixture by migratory infiltration of nomadic peoples from the northeast. As the high-pasturage ones now exist, they are recognizably Mongoloid, but exhibit a startling diversity of type. Many of them closely resemble Amerindians. A series of photographs in my possession of nomadic pastoralists from widely separated districts of Tibet illustrates both their diversity and this resemblance. Some look like blood kin of Sitting Bull, and Indians of the type from which the stylized Indian head has been developed; others look like Haida, Macaw, and tribes of the Pacific Northwest. Suydam Cutting said that those he met reminded him of the Navaho (Cutting 1940:187).

Some of them have been described as "burly" and larger than other Tibetans. This is, I believe, an illusion, due more to bulky clothing and their self-assurance and arrogance, which they wear like a garment, than to any difference in actual size. Indeed, those from higher elevations (15,000–17,000 feet) and particularly *Byang Pa* and *mGo Log* whom I have met were small, though compact and wiry. However, those members of tribes near the upper knee of the Yellow River, who live at relatively low altitudes (12,000 feet and up), are strikingly large and well-built.

Without exception they are weather-beaten. They are the ones least sheltered from all the weather extremes of the Tibetan plateau. Scorched by sunshine of increased ultraviolet ray intensity, they are deeply tanned; they are grimed as well with oily soot from sheep manure and cow-chip fires, and repeatedly greased with butter. The scorching June sunshine, reflected from snow fields, is alternated with frost and biting cold, and in winter, temperatures drop to —20 or —40° F if the nights are clear and still. Temperatures rise with the wind, but the assault of cold on sense and body is then amplified by wind which carries snow, dust, grit, and even pebbles against man and beast with such force that it is impossible to travel against the storm.

The hardihood which so strikingly characterizes the *aBrog Pa* does not come solely in response to ecological challenge. There are many other influences which help toughen them, but storm and stress have certainly habituated them to a disdainfully studied disregard of weather. They will stand barefooted in slush that is half snow and half mud, seemingly unaware of discomfort, except that they occasionally lift one foot or the other to hold it against a leg for warming. I have seen men roping packs on yak with their right arms, shoulders, and half their torsos bare in zero weather. When a hailstorm is at its worst, they huddle under a big felt raincoat, like a half-shelter, drinking their tea as cheerfully as though it were a picnic in the sunshine.

Ownership and Social Structure

Men and women such as these own and tend their livestock; secure and even proud that their ownership is unquestioned and unqualified by an ultimate claim of the state or other higher authority, such as applies to fields worked by the tillers of the soil, who mostly hold and till their fields on the basis of usufruct rather than ownership. No such ultimate claims of ownership challenge the reality of possession with which the nomadic pastoralists own their herds, though there are many instances of livestock being committed to the care of herders, on either a sharecrop or hired-help basis. In central Tibet, government cattle and sheep are farmed out in large numbers, yet even there livestock possessed by the herder belong with finality to him *only*. This gives him a degree of assurance which the peasant farmer in the same area can never have concerning his fields. Fields on the hoof not only have current mobility, but, because of changes from the past running through the future, have elusiveness as to place and variability as to numbers, which make it virtually impossible to deed them for all time as endowments to monasteries, or as fiefs to vassals, as has been done so often in Tibetan history with soil fields and the peasants who till them.

The manner in which this ownership is spread throughout the nomadic pastoralist society indicates a great deal about the structure of the society, emphasizing the worth and ranking of the individual and suggesting much concerning the position of women within the society.

The ownership of livestock lies essentially with the tenthold, or family. Normally, the oldest male represents the family and makes most of the decisions concerning herd management, disposal of annual yield, seasonal movement, and representation of the family in the community. Decision making does not, however, give him preferential ownership, for all members of the family have rights within that ownership. At any point his decisions may be challenged by other members of the tenthold.

Such challenge comes most frequently from the wife who is mistress of the tent. If, in an extended family, the challenge comes from one or more of the sons, it is, in effect, the first step toward fragmentation into nuclear-family units. The life expectancy of the extended family rarely lasts beyond the death, or retirement, of the elder generation. When the eldest son marries, the extended family usually has its first break-off, although there is a tradition that: "The family should not break up while the parents are still alive." Two reasons for fragmentation have special validity: (a) two women cannot function efficiently and without friction as comistresses in a tent economy; (b) division of the production wealth of a family is much more easily effected when that wealth is livestock fields than when it is soil fields, particularly as each member of the family can make a tally of what his or her portion should be.

Because the breakup of parental, extended families into nuclear families is so commonplace, usually effected in a matter-of-fact way with relatively slight emotional turmoil or any sense of violation of the proprieties, and because the accompanying distribution of wealth is easily made on the basis of long-standing consensus as to how much belongs to whom, the relationship of the new family, or families, with the older parent family continues to be amicable. They remain in the same encampment, there is much mutual help, with frequent sharing of roles, throughout the nomadic pastoral routine.

From her normal position of being the sole tent mistress, with an equal portion right, most frequently it is the wife who challenges male decisions. In my own experience, when buying a sheep for meat, for example, repeatedly I have had an agreed-upon sale vetoed by the tent wife, arguing that the animal was of more importance in herd management, or of more value for the wool it would produce, and making her argument stick—leaving me with no sheep. Butter or cheese, at least in small quantities, is always sold by the tent wife with slight reference to her husband's opinion.

Among the siblings, each one has right to an equal share of the common wealth, and the father and mother each have a right to two such units. In a family of six—parents, two sons, and two daughters—when the eldest son marries, he receives one-eighth of the livestock fields of his family, but, since a bride brings with her the dowry of her share of her family's wealth, that will not be the sole economic base of the new nuclear tenthold. Each of the other siblings at marriage also gets one-eighth. When all marry, or leave, the father and mother still have four-eighths of the original production wealth of the family.

Ideally, at the death of the parents, this wealth should be devoted to religious observances—payment to lamas and monks for chanting services and the making of large offerings to the shrines and monasteries. In actual practice, though a considerable portion is spent in this manner, much of it is divided among the siblings. A great deal depends on their piety and how amicable the relations between the parental extended family and the split-off nuclear families and in-laws have been. Habitual relationships with the nearest monastery, and the promptness with which monastery managers arrive on the scene when death has taken place, also have an influence. As with all paradigms—particularly those applying to aspects of social structure and interpersonal relationships—there are an almost infinite number of variations in any predicated norm.

The family may be either monogamous, polygynous, or polyandrous, though by far the great majority of families are monogamous, and in each form ownership distribution exhibits significant differences. Within the pattern of family ownership various aspects of individual ownership, or, at least, prior claim, are to be found; moreover, in virtually every case female ownership rights are of considerable complexity.

Polygynous family structure has a peculiarly divisive effect on livestock ownership. Except in the case of sororal polygyny, or the rather rare mother-daughter form, no attempt is made to preserve a one-tent ownership of livestock. Two sisters possibly can function as comistresses of the tent—though even then, control of the churn may pose greater problems than sexual jealousy—but no man in his senses should expect to keep two nonsibling women in the same tent. Polygyny is only found in tentholds of considerable affluence, for it involves setting up two tents and dividing the livestock correspondingly.

Usually, it is an older man of wealth and position taking a younger wife. Fondness for a young servant girl with whom he has slept, somewhat rarely for polygynous marriages are rather rare but sleeping with servant girls is quite common, will induce him to make her his second wife according to form. This involves setting up a second tent, known as the "little" tent, having its own separate herd and management. Normally this little tent has a smaller economic base in livestock than the "big" tent of the older wife. Unless the second wife brings some wealth of her own, that base consists of one-half of the husband's share in the big tent, together with whatever personal wealth he may claim. If he is a very wealthy man, this may be quite ample, but in any case, he needs to leave some of his wealth with the big tent as working capital to ensure his leadership in management of its interests.

The polygynous husband is a man with two tentholds to each of which he sustains a similar relationship and by the terms of that relationship he is the master of each tent. His sexual relationship to his first wife may or may not lapse, but his formal relationship to the affairs and management of the big tent remains in full force. At each move the two tents are set up next to each other and a close reciprocity of mutual aid between the two is maintained, for kinship entails special attitudes of helpfulness and involvement. Of the two tent families, the little one is likely to be nuclear, but the big tent frequently is extended in structure, for older-generation relatives and dependents may be a part of it. Though complicated in structure and not very common, this polygynous bifamily arrangement is more stable than the average monogamous family and less subject to fragmentation than the usual run of polyandrous families, for the economic structure is interlocking and correspondingly strong.

The polyandrous family is somewhat more common, but is less resistant to fragmentation and consists usually of two or more brothers sharing the same wife, but other arrangements, including father-son cohusbands, are not unknown. Quite frequently, two brothers decide not to divide the family herds and, since both sense and experience are against there being two tent mistresses, they agree to share one wife. This arrangement often begins when an older brother allows sexual access to his wife by his adolescent younger brother in the effort to keep the economic base of the tent intact. Such fraternal polyandrous marriages are quite unstable, due to sexual rather than economic reasons. The younger brother tires of the older woman and wants a younger one for his own wife, and inevitable breakup of the arrangement takes place. Occasionally, it is the wife who takes a special liking to one of the two brothers and then, in effect, pushes out the other one, who, nevertheless, takes with him his share of the livestock.

The "called-in-son-in-law" monogamous marriage is of particular interest, for it also is devised to preserve family wealth intact and results in an extended family. It occurs mostly in affluent tentholds. When a family has only one daughter, or when all but one of the daughters have married and left, a son-in-law—usually from a family of less wealth—is brought in as surrogate son. If he has a lineage "bone" name or even "house" name, he discards it and takes the lineage name of his wife, as a son of the tent, but unlike a real son, he does not have the right to set up his own tenthold apart from the one of his wife's parents. It is assumed that mother and daughter can function in harmony as comistresses of the one tent. If the father dies early, the family may become polyandrous, with mother and daughter as cowives. As an extended polyandrous family, it is quite secure against fragmentation and may only be changed in structure by attrition when both parents have died.

In these variations of family structure, economic considerations appear to take precedence over commonly cited reasons—sanctioned sexual relations and security for the children—for the institution of marriage. This may be because: (a) there is a considerable degree of sexual license, both before and after marriage, and thus sexual experimentation and satisfaction is not dependent on formally sanctioned arrangements presupposing exclusivity; (b) there is a dearth of children, for the birth rate is very low, and children are in demand. An unmarried mother is, if anything, more desirable than one without children, and adoption of children by childless families takes place frequently. On the one hand, the need for a compact between the sexually associating man and woman to insure care of progeny is not pressing. On the other hand, the need for a compact to manage the business of a tent is imperative. It requires a partnership between a man and a woman—each in an exclusive role—which is of reasonable stability. Thus, basic economic factors, carefully calculated in the head count of livestock, are of great importance.

Within the framework of tent-family ownership of livestock, there is both opportunity and sanction for private ownership, or claim to use of individual animals. It may come about in a number of ways. Raiding, hunting, guiding caravans, or special individual skills—veterinarian know-how, fine weaving, tailoring, and bootmaking—are ways whereby members of the tenthold come into possession of personal wealth. In some instances it is livestock—a lamb or calf given for services, or stock brought back as one rider's share in a raid. It can also be the price gained for skins or furs, a pod of musk, or a rack of stag antlers in the velvet, but always it is individually owned wealth—quickly changed into livestock. Individual animals belonging to individual members of the family do not come into any reckoning or dividing of family wealth.

In addition to outright ownership, by continuous use of, or specialized personal association with certain animals—particularly those which may be ridden—members of the family gain preferential claim to use of certain animals and can protest sale of them. Another member of the family, for example, will ask permission to saddle or use a certain horse or yak in acknowledgment of this loosely defined but generally accepted claim.

Ownership rights of women, both within the patterns of family ownership and of individual ownership, are of particular interest. Male and female siblings inherit equally. The eldest son and the youngest daughter have the same inheritance right. What the latter takes with her as dowry to another tenthold at marriage remains, in a sense, hers. In divorce, she is entitled to the dowry by head count. If the tenthold has prospered during the years of her association and has increased its livestock holdings, she is entitled to a share of that increment, for by her role as tent mistress she has contributed to it. Ownership rights of the women are strengthened by the very special relationship they have with the stock. Caring for it at birth, looking after its young, and, particularly, milking it are done only by women. Over the disposal of milk-producing stock the woman of the tent has a power of veto, which she can press with emotional intensity.

Ownership of livestock has so far been discussed on two levels, the family and the individual. At the next higher level of the encampment—in many respects the analogue of the hamlet in an agricultural society—there is no observable trace of communal ownership of livestock, except in a temporary form when the encampment has to receive or pay livestock. Livestock collected by levy from the tent families of the encampment are held as the herd of the encampment until they can be delivered in payment, and the herd received in payment is similarly held until the stock can be divided among the tentholds.

The encampment itself is not a prime level of social structure in pastoral society, but is a by-product of security requirements or topography. In many districts it does not exist because each tenthold camps by itself at grazing-exploitation distance—the area within which livestock can be pastured daily without competing with livestock from other tents. Where it does exist, it varies in size from a small circle of five or six tents to a circle of as many as eighty tents. During the seasonal displacement, it may change according to topography, coalescing into existence on a plain or in a wide valley, and breaking up into individual tent sites in rough country. Wherever it exists in permanent form, it is organized with a headman—usually the wealthiest or *most able* individual—and sometimes the encampment is known as his *Ru sKor* (tent circle). He takes charge of decision making by the men of the encampment and represents the encampment in dealing with higher authority.

The next higher level of social structure is the *TSHo Ba* (group ones)—sometimes also called *SHog Pa* (wing ones)—which is a somewhat amorphous lineage grouping. It presumably is related to a common ancestor from whom it takes its name, and it is, actually, somewhat like a clan in the process of decay. Virtually all that remains of what once was undoubtedly a powerful and cohesive ingroup is the tradition of gathering for certain ceremonies, of a military or head-count character. Where it is best known, the *TSHo Ba* is one of two or more segments of a tribe, but due to the fluid and mobile character of Tibetan society *TSHo Ba* members may be found scattered throughout a number of tribes. As presently known, there is no *TSHo Ba* ownership of livestock.

At the tribal level of social *and political* organization there is also no form of permanent communal ownership of stock, but as in the encampment, during the process of receiving or paying indemnities, temporary holding in a common tribal herd does take place. Tribal decision may specify, moreover, what kind of stock can be owned or may require certain numbers in certain categories. In some areas it is forbidden to breed yak-common-cattle hybrids or even to keep them; also, in most tribes, as defense policy, there are requirements which make mandatory the keeping of a certain number of good riding horses per tent.

Under whichever label it is known, the tribe is historically the basic political organization of the nomadic pastoralists. This is so within the structure of national organization in central Tibet; in larger autonomous domains such as *Sa sKya* and various "kingships," or throughout eastern Tibet, where—until the Chinese communist take-over—various groupings were under Chinese claims of overlordship, but possessed virtual autonomy. In this latter area, where the tribes retained their strongest and clearest political characteristics, they varied in size from those of less than a hundred tents to others of several thousand. In *A mDo*, the *gSer rTa mGo Log* tribe numbered over 6000 tents even after a split-off of nearly two thousand tents that, under the name *A mDo sTod Ma*, moved into central Tibet and settled at the headwaters of the *Nag CHu*, where they led an existence of virtual independence. In the northwest, the *aBrong Ba* (wild-yak ones), a tribe of over 300 tents of the "north-plain" nomads, in theory are under the jurisdiction of the *Ru THog rDZong,* but are largely autonomous and known by their tribal name. Even a pastoral tribe such as the *PHu Ma mTSHo Byang THang Pa* (*Phu Ma* lake north-plain ones), which is relatively close to Lhasa itself, and which actually pays a livestock head tax every three years, is yet known by its original tribal designation. Nomadic pastoralist communities have in many areas become identified with administrative districts of the central Tibetan government, yet the tribe, as a district and very early unit of political power, with varying degrees of autonomy and quasi, or real, independence, is the principal power entity. Pridefully, it has its own name, identity, and a strong sense of its rights, maintained both by force and evasive mobility. In some areas under pressure, it may retain little more than a name and vestigial powers; elsewhere, it is a strong organization. As thus defined, and qualified, the term "tribe" is used throughout this book.

At all effective levels of social and political structure there exists a special form of offertory guardian-ownership wherein a family, encampment, or tribe makes an offering of livestock to the gods. Any animal may be so offered, but usually it is a male yak, ceremoniously presented to the gods. Known as *lHa gYag* (god yak), these animals are set completely free and may not be used or even handled by anyone. They are free to go as they please, but if they follow the community in its seasonal move it is a good omen. If they choose to wander off by themselves, no effort is made to control them, but the community does seek to protect them from harm or outside interference and, thus, communally acts as guardian of these livestock of the gods. The offering is a gesture of piety by the community, and of self-interest in anticipation of blessing. Yet it seems also to be an unwitting making of amends, and an acknowledgment that domestication of the very livestock on which pastoralism depends, and which, by their mobility, make that society nomadic, is an infringement of natural rights as first willed by the gods.

5

Care of Livestock

LIVESTOCK CARE IS, in sum, the provision of pasture, protection, and veterinarian care. Each task makes special demands on the individual and the community. None is simplistic, nor a plodding performance of a set routine, but a succession of varied responses to exigencies.

Pasturing and Seasonal Routine

Of the three tasks, pasturing is of primary importance, and spatially is conditioned by such things as topography, quality of soil, sufficiency of moisture, and degree of insolation, which affect the growth of grass—that covering of the earth which is the herders' primary concern. Pasturing is synchronized in sequence with the sprouting, growth, and maturation of vegetation. Synchronization, in turn, imposes diurnal and seasonal routines on communities and individuals, making them both pastoral and nomadic. Pastoral activity varies in intensity according to the kind, but there is no outright pause resembling the farmer's winter, for care of livestock is a round-the-clock all-season occupation.

Functionally, the pastoralist grass-growth year does not begin in midwinter, but its coming is heralded, in early spring, by the first pale-green sprouts, which appear with special richness in the cropped-bare, heavily fertilized pastures of the winter quarters. There, the winter-killed hay, yellow and dry, has been eaten down to the roots, and the sprouts promise some nourishment. Yet there is little substance and nourishment in them and for the first few days when the stock "have new grass between their teeth" they lose rather than gain flesh.

It is, moreover, a time of special threat. The stock are starved to the bone—gaunt skeletons draped with ragged winter coats—having little strength or resistance. One spring snowfall, covering the grass for only two or three days, can mean the death of scores, and a spring blizzard can leave the pastoralist with no herds at all making him a virtual pauper without "fields." For days, the ebbing

31

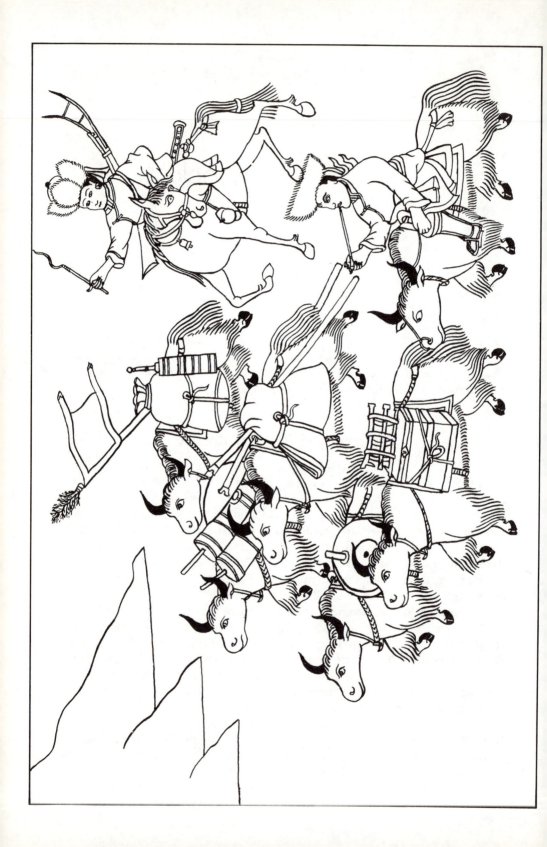

strength of the stock and the new grass, responding to the sudden pull of spring-time sunshine, are precariously balanced. There is little the herdsman can do, yet that little may save many of his stock. Among those tribes that have sod, or otherwise structured, winter quarters where hay may be stored, carefully calculated handfuls are distributed to the weakest animals, and the herds are gently guided toward the nearest sheltered sunny slopes, where grass sprouts and darkens fastest and new-fallen snow melts soonest.

Signaled by sprouting and darkening grass that at last brings saving strength, the functional year of the nomadic pastoralists starts with the first move of the season: from the winter quarters to the nearest area where the grass has been untouched since the previous spring. Normally, three moves is the very minimum and eight a maximum, but emergencies may cause a community to move a dozen times a year. At the other extreme, one tribe in southern Tibet, for example, moves once every three years and builds half-cave, half-sod houses at each move, yet because it has no persisting link with agricultural communities, it is considered *aBrog CHen* (great high pasturage).

When a community moves out of winter quarters to begin the seasonal search for the best pasturage, the families retain their winter-quarters location relationships. If they have been organized as an encampment—commonly called "tent circle"—they continue that pattern of placement throughout each of the moves; if they have camped separately, yet having a neighborhood relationship as a group, they maintain the same pattern and neighborly relationship: within long earshot of each other, or at least within a few minutes ride. Occasionally, as they move, the pattern is adjusted to topography. Where it is steppe-like, or wide valleys, the tent neighborhood groups in a circle, but where it consists of narrow ravines and sharp ridges, the tents may be scattered along a valley and its connecting side valleys—keeping relatively close, however, so that their herdsmen meet during the day, or combine in cooperative herding.

The date of the first move varies according to both latitude and altitude. Sometime between the middle of April to as late as the end of May, whenever reports concerning the growth of grass are favorable, local soothsaying lamas are asked to divine and fix a date which is auspicious according to the horoscope. Where security is a pressing problem, attempts are made, not always successfully, to keep the selected day secret until the very time the move is made. Thus, in the give and take of conversation, it is not considered good form to ask questions about the dates of community movement. Secrecy is often so well maintained that a traveler, having full assurance of finding an encampment at the end of a day's ride, finds only an abandoned campsite.

Reconnaissance to ascertain trail conditions—and checking grazing conditions in the area—precedes any move. In a tribe near the upper knee of the Yellow River, with whom I lived and traveled for several months, it was customary to send scouts in a wide sweep to the very limits of the tribal range to make sure that raiders were not lurking nearby, and on the day of the move, two or three riders from each encampment maintained a protective watch along the route.

The first move in spring is the one in which the community is at the greatest disadvantage and most vulnerable. The stock are weak, and there are numbers of the newly born—calves, lambs, colts, and even puppies—that require special care. Births sometimes take place along the trail, and it is not uncommon to see riders arrive with lambs in the saddlebags or a struggling calf across the front of the saddle. Cattle, sheep, and horses all have the hunger of the half-starved. As soon as fresh pastures beyond the grazed-over winter pastures are reached, some of the animals, tempted by the lush new grass, tend to break away from the herd, as they hungrily snatch mouthfuls. Such purposeful laggards make herding doubly difficult, as the tent family, and sections of encampment and tribe, confusedly straggle toward the first of the grazing-cycle campsites.

The move is relatively short, for the stock are in no condition to make a trek much beyond the limits of the grazed-to-the-roots area near the winter quarters. Furthermore, such nearby sites have an earlier growth of grass than other areas of the community range. Confused, slow, and lasting most of the day, the first move covers only a few miles—though many hours.

The length of stay in the first of the grazing-cycle sites is seldom more than ten days. The grass of thicker growth and darker green is hunger-satisfying, strength-giving nourishment, yet only an inch or two high and soon cropped short by famished stock. Within those few days—unless a late and heavy snowfall comes—the precarious balance between dwindling livestock vigor and the growing grass changes and tips toward certainty that for the year starvation is ended and that the animals will grow fat as the grass ripens. Later successive moves are carried out with less confusion, and, with no problem of lagging stock, the rate of movement becomes that of any well-driven caravan. Each successive stay is lengthened as the grass grows higher and more nutritious, and in the early fall, when it is belly high and heavy with seed, a community may stay as long as a month in one spot.

Haymaking: The Pattern of Movement

Following the growth of grass takes the nomadic pastoralists from lower to higher, and then back to lower, elevations. In midsummer they are camped in the highest pastures of their range—near the limits of vegetation and the scree slopes of the high mountains. In early fall they are back at lower levels, not far from winter quarters. Caring for the herds, they follow the grass in its growth and, for some, this care extends to preserving grass for winter feed. This attempt is made late in September to early in October. Only communities which have in their winter quarters safely enclosed storage areas, attempt haying; storage is more of a problem than cutting and curing, because winter starvation turns stock into pilfering thieves.

The manpower problem is acute at this season, for such activities as herding, milking, and buttermaking and cheesemaking must continue, while as much manpower as possible should be diverted to a crash program of cutting, curing, and storing the maximum amount of hay. Fortunately, during this period grazing problems are minimal. In a camp surrounded by seed-heavy grass that may be belly high the livestock can be kept close to the tent and yet be well-fed. They are lazy and fat, as if with half-satiated appetites, they crop the grass tops. One person in a family may stay with the tent and herds, while all other members, with what help they can hire, move to the winter quarters, where for about fifteen days they make hay of the grass that grows with special thickness in the vicinity. It is a time of intense and unremitting effort; as the hay is cut, cured, and twisted into bunches for easy handling, packing, and storage. Work lasts from dawn until late at night if moonlight favors.

Not all nomadic pastoralists attempt to make hay. By preference, or by stubbornly maintained tradition, many trust to animal fat and flesh accumulated throughout the grazing cycle to carry the herds through the starvation and cold of winter. They may have heavier losses than those who prepare hay for emergency feeding, yet they proudly boast that they are fully nomadic, neither harvesting nor having fixed winter quarters. When winter comes, they stay wherever the grass is long and there is sheltering topography.

Winter quarters and making hay are, indeed, steps toward sedentary agriculture, even though fixed habitation is of limited duration. Whatever the nature of the winter-quarters structure—sod, adobe, dug-in pits, caves or even dung-daubed wattle walls—it does necessitate breaking the sod, and nomads who winter in such structures are sensitive about the fact. Making hay results in development of rudimentary family right to usufruct of the soil (Ekvall 1954a). Each tenthold comes to have its own permanent exclusive right to cut hay on certain hayfields near the winter quarters. This resembles, in fact, the usufruct basis on which the peasant works his fields. It differs radically from the manner in which the nomadic community holds right to the grassland where herds are pastured. Haying—the cutting, in particular—is also disturbingly atypical to the norm of pastoralist activity, and many a nomad prefers to let hired peasants do the cutting—which should be done by the teeth of his stock—while he takes charge of twisting and storing the hay.

Winter campsites being low and, thus, close to agricultural communities, workers from the latter migrate to help with the haying, bringing harvesting skills, earning good wages, and having a much desired taste of herders' diet, with its abundance of butter, cheese, and meat. In shared experience, both spatially and in culture change, the two societies—nomadic pastoralist and sedentary agriculturalist—are in close proximity. In may also be the first step whereby a poverty-stricken peasant gets a foothold among nomadic pastoralists, eventually becoming one of them.

Winter quarters and haymaking, as a culture-trait complex, is an extension of the function of pasturing the herds, assuring sufficient grass when needed, yet its real significance is that, by "settling down" temporarily and reaping the product of the soil, the aBrog CHen (great high pasturage) or the "true nomads," also take the first step from nomadic pastoralism toward sedentary agriculturalism.

After the hay is stored, the workers rejoin their home communities. A month or so later, winter cold brings herders and herds down to the shelter of lower levels and windbreak topography. What remains of following the grass in order to fatten stock is the last phase, which is to conserve accumulated flesh by as much protection against cold and as little movement as is feasible. Pasturing is reduced to turning the stock loose late in the cold morning, after the sun has freed winter-killed grass of frost, to stand or move like zombies, satisfying hunger, with little relish, on dried-out yellow stalks.

Pasturing and Daily Routines

Each successive stage of the pasturing cycle creates differences in diurnal routines of community members. In all activity there exists a basic division, or assignment, of male and female roles. The exclusiveness of each role ranges from the absolute to a point where there appears to be virtual free interchange—action in which men or women act together, or with no apparent reference to maleness or femaleness of role. Butchering and the handling and use of weapons are good examples of exclusively male roles; milking and churning are good examples of exclusively female roles; but other activities such as tethering stock and packing and unpacking in a move appear to be equally men's and women's work, according to need. Close observation, nevertheless, will show some preponderance of either role, manifested in relative frequency of participation or in scope or manner of performance. The pattern of action for the individual which thus results is obviously a reflection of generally accepted and observed norms. As in every society, there are atypical or abnormal patterns which arise by accident from emergency requirements or because of individual nonconformism.

During the entire year, action by the individual is inexorably related to the changing length of the day because stock grazing habits are geared to daylight. With few exceptions stock only graze in daylight, even if risk and security considerations would permit leaving them loose at night.

At the winter solstice the pastoralist's day is a short and lazy one, stock being turned loose as late as 9:00 A.M. to wander slowly by themselves to nearby pasturage. There is little earlier activity such as milking, and letting them out of the pens is simple. By 5:00 P.M., or earlier, it is time to gather them in, but there is little milking and time-consuming tethering. In mid-June, however, the stock are pulling restlessly on their tether lines before 4:00 A.M. and, for at least an hour prior to that, there is much activity—milking, getting ready for the day's herding, and attention to other chores. The workday starts before dawn and tethering the stock goes on until dusk is turning to night, before the members of the family can gather around the fire for a very late evening meal, with the beginning of another day only four or five hours away. The summer day of the nomadic pastoralists, is relentlessly long—at high hot noon, they are sleepwalkers, drugged with drowsiness—and filled with tasks that give little pause for rest.

Description of three days selected from the pastoralist's year show how male and female roles interact in individual and communal activity in so caring for livestock that it gains maximum condition from the *rTSwa KHa* (grass part) of the *aBrog*. It also shows how effort-tempo is conditioned by daylight, for fields on the hoof, like soil fields, are also atuned to the light and warmth of the sun.

No day is more representative and filled with activity than the spring day of the first move. Long before daybreak men and women are busy sorting and packing. The men take care of the chests which hold religious treasures—books, images, offering bowls, incense urns, and scrolls; they balance sacks of grain and other foodstuffs so the loads will be stable; they bale and rope hides, sheepskins, and felts and set out the pack and riding saddles. The women wrap kitchen gear; clean churns, kettles, and water buckets for loading; boil tea for the hasty breakfast that may be the only meal until late at night; sort and pack surplus clothing and footwear; carefully wrap the slabs of dried clay or specially selected stones with which the hearth will be made at the new campsite; and fill all spare fuel sacks with dried droppings which are plentiful and at hand in the cattle pens.

The tent, which is heavy, requiring all available manpower, must then come down. Both men and women work, with seemingly no preferential role, but the men bring greater strength to heavy aspects of the joint task. The same principle holds true in saddling cattle and horses; it is done by both men and women with equal know-how, but the men attend to a final tightening of girths. Men do most of the loading, for a man can more easily heave a half-load against one side of the packsaddle, and hold it there with his shoulder while making the hitch. If the woman cannot heave the other half in place on her side, she can at least hold up the half already tied, while the man heaves the other half in place. Both then pull the ropes tight over the load and fasten them to the girth.

Loading completed and stock and baggage oxen turned loose, men and women equally, with scant regard of role, ride herd, round up laggards, adjust unbalanced loads, and meet the emergencies of the trail, though the scouts of the community, who guard passes and high points overlooking the trail, are weapons-carrying males. It is a man also who gathers and attaches the tether ropes to his saddle and, when near the new campsite, rides ahead to stretch the tether ropes before the loaded oxen arrive. Tethering is the job of anyone—man or woman—who gets a hand on the nose-ring rope, and in unloading and setting up the tent both men and women work together, with the same nuanced difference that marked taking it down.

Once the tent ropes have been pulled taut, male and female roles become more clearly differentiated. Sorting the family possessions and stacking them within the tent is a common task, but the man takes care of the things *he* packed, sets up the family altar with a token offering, cuts the sod—with appropriate prayers to the "earth lords"—to make the ashpit for the hearth, and then takes a look at the stock to make sure they have not strayed. Meanwhile, the woman unpacks kitchen equipment, makes sure the sacks of fuel are under shelter in a corner of the tent, sets up the stove of stone or slabs of dried clay, gets water, starts boiling tea, hurriedly milks ewes and cows that need it, and, if there is enough milk for churning, starts the making of the day's butter.

There is never a pause throughout a day which, if trail time were short and the straggling herds did not stop altogether, sees the most difficult displacement of the year well completed by dusk. Sometimes, however, the herds scatter and stragglers get in so late in the night that a day which began before dawn may run through until another dawn—the forerider of the sun—at 3:00 A.M. During this day pasturing is very much *ad hoc*. Cattle graze as they can on the trail; grass around the new campsite is comparatively lush and there is little tendency to stray, but, as they are in a new place and unfamiliar with tether-line locations and night-herd stands, they are rounded up at early dusk. Such are the crowding tasks for both men and women in the long day of the first grazing-cycle move.

A nomadic pastoralist's day in midsummer may be an even longer one, but full of a more ordered routine with—unless disaster strikes—less improvised response to emergency and more planned care of livestock—a herder's, not a mover's, day. It too starts long before the morning star begins to fade. Though other activity, concerned with herd management, harvesting animal products, and the techniques of their utilization (all described later), bulks large in the day's routine, the focus of activity is to make possible the maximum of grazing under optimum circumstances so that the lush pastures of midsummer may be transformed into animal reserves of flesh and fat, stored up against the cold and starvation of midwinter.

The women start the tea boiling, and then hurry to the cows so they can be turned loose with the other cattle. This is the moment—if any—when prayers are said before the family altar, and the ritual offerings are renewed by the man of the tent; then all gather for a hasty drinking of "early tea"—a few minutes pause around the tent fire—as plans for the day are made and tasks assigned.

Whoever is to be away all day with the herds sorts and packs noonday tea equipment and supplies—kettles, bellows, fuel, tea, tsamba,* butter, cheese, and any available delicacies such as sausage and yoghurt—and selects the mounts to be used—horse or yak—and saddles them. The women pour the morning milking from the cows into the churn, then sort out the milkable ewes and tie them head to head in a long double row for later milking, giving what help they can to man's work of unhobbling cattle and horses.

The horses of the community are usually driven in one consolidated herd to the very fringes of pasturage which can be exploited on a daily basis, for they need the very best grazing and can move quickly to where the grass is untouched. Horses should not graze with the cattle for they are in some danger. The stated theme of a legend "enmity of the horse and yak" is something quite real and is particularly true when cows have calved or it is mating time. One toss of a horned head can .mean a disemboweled horse. Cattle, as ruminants, fill up quickly and then rest to chew the cud, and so graze with less oversight nearer the tents.

After the horse herd has started and the cattle have scattered slowly, the women milk the ewes and then turn loose the lambs—kept from their mothers during the night in portable corrals—and also unhobble the calves so they too can find their mothers. The cows will be brought back later to the tent for the noon milking. The hybrid cows, having no calves and having transferred something of maternal affection to the women who milk them, will come of their own accord and when their udders are full, may even follow the women into the tents. After being milked, they will be driven out again to graze and lazily chew the cud in the hot sun.

In the tasks directly concerned with the primary care of livestock, to make possible the maximum of grazing under optimum circumstances, men and women participate with what appears to be a free exchange of roles as both sexes ride

---

* Flour made by roasting barley until it pops and then grinding it.

herd on the sheep or help each other round up cattle, yet invariably it is the men who, armed and mounted, take the horse herd to the peripheral grazing grounds and guard that herd—of all livestock, the most vulnerable to a raid—throughout the day. It is the women, however, who deal with cows, ewes, and their young, as they carefully keep the requirements of grazing care, milking opportunity, and the sustenance needs of calves and lambs in balance.

The exigencies of herding in midsummer are extremely demanding. The stock are well-fleshed enough to be vigorous, but not fat enough to be lazy. The mating urge and the desire to wander are strong. The yak and *mDZo* cows have a particular impulse to seek the spot where they dropped last year's calves. Insect pests keep the herds in uneasy motion throughout the sunlight hours, and thunderstorms may stampede them. In all the varied activity which summer weather, harvest chores, and utilization of animal products require, each member of the tent family must be ready to drop whatever he is doing to saddle and ride after straying stock. The long summer day often seems filled with those alarms.

The day in late fall or early winter when the tent community moves back into winter quarters, or to one of several alternate campsites in the lowest, most sheltered part of its territory, if it has no permanent winter quarters, marks the close of the grazing-cycle year. Like the first move, but in reverse, it marks an end and a beginning, the end of primary emphasis on pasturing to make the stock fat against future privation, for they are already at maximum condition in stored-up, laid-on flesh-fat—"two fingers of fat to show" when the skin is cut on a butchered carcass—and the beginning of a conservation process by careful herding on vegetation past maturation and slowly losing nutritive value as it turns yellow and dry in its own recession of growth, in the cold of winter. In the routine of the move the tasks of men and women resemble those of the spring move, but there is more order. The animals are both strong and lazy with fat and may be driven with little trouble and few spilled loads. There also are no helpless young requiring special attention; all march strongly, almost as if celebrating the triumph of pastoral endeavor, along familiar trails into well-known haunts. Of their own accord they crowd into the pens of the winter quarters where men and women share, with only nuanced differences of role, the tasks of settling in for the winter. On the men's side of the tent, the right-hand one looking in from the door, having first laid aside his weapons, conveniently near, on the stacked-up loads along the side wall of the tent, the eldest male sets up the altar and spreads the offerings. The woman, meanwhile, puts together the tent stove, starts the fire, and brings water for tea. They are back home at a base where, though still pastoralists, many other activities will take up their time throughout the long winter nights and short winter days and where they are appreciably less nomadic than at any other time.

Protection

Care of livestock requires varieties and degrees of protection which the farmer seldom, if ever, has to furnish for his soil fields. Men have battled to protect their *lands* from invasion and conquest, but such effort comes but rarely, and in the context of national struggle. In addition to participation in such defensive struggle—though his mobility often affords him escape or gives him evasion capability—the pastoralist must give his livestock protection against many dangers. The primary one, which has the greatest impact on patterns of behavior and the use of time, comes from other nomadic pastoralists. They may be enemies of long standing, seeking to even old scores; they also may be individuals or groups who, in a sense, were neutral until opportunity gave them the chance to steal or, by the threat or use of force, to drive away the ever temptingly mobile fields on the hoof.

Raiding for livestock occurs all over Tibet, but the scale and frequency vary greatly. Some communities experience little more than the occasional theft of a single sheep. Elsewhere, raiders are a constant threat, particularly during those seasons when horses are in good condition to make possible fast riding. Late winter is generally safe but early fall, a time of danger.

Against the threat of danger the response is constant vigilance. When the community is on the move, scouts are sent ahead to the hilltops and passes, and there is instant suspicion of armed and mounted men, particularly if they do not have baggage animals as a sign of innocuous travel or are without the many loaded oxen of a trade caravan (Ekvall 1952: 159–161). Most men of the encampment sleep in small shelters or under felt cover-alls on the rim of the tent circle. Their sleep is, indeed, much broken by wakefulness and shouting and the deep baying of encampment dogs, which have their own role in guarding the herds at night. These dogs, more or less of mastiff breed, are noted for ferocity, and in their watchdog function play a special role in the culture which will be discussed in another context.

As vigilance is response to threat, so action and weaponry are response to danger. The men who act as lookouts along the trail set their noon campfires on hilltops and other vantage points when they guard the herds on the outer fringes of the community pasturage, and sleep lightly, in broken snatches, throughout short summer nights, always armed and prepared to use their arms. Indeed, when the nights are moonless or stormy, the noise of men hallooing and dogs barking is occasionally increased by gunfire accompanied by shouted defiance to thieves, lurking in the dark somewhere beyond the encampment rim.

Menace and response are linked to phases of the moon. Only when the night is white with the moonlight of high altitudes (at its strongest I have read newsprint in that brightness) do men and dogs sleep. The encampment then becomes quiet, except for the sounds of the stock shifting slightly and the labored breathing of cud-chewing bovines.

Each individual senses responsibility when danger threatens the herds, but action comes most frequently from herders on guard. With the exception of girls and women, all—even teen-age boys—on this duty are armed. Each tent possesses firearms. Even the poorest has one or two muzzle-loading matchlocks, and a tent of modest affluency has at least one breech-loading rifle. To defend the herds, gunfire can come from any of the daylong herder campfires surrounding the tent community. Occasionally, a woman may be in such a group, but being unarmed, she is out of place. Women by themselves are responsible for pasturing cattle or sheep within the periphery, but engage in no direct armed response. When a girl or woman is involved in direct action, she does everything possible—such as saddling and unhobbling horses and looking after cooking gear—to free the men for warning of the community or for pursuit.

In addition to *ad hoc* individual and group reaction there exists in each tent community a spontaneous yet institutionalized collective action known as *Ra mDaa* (fence arrow)—somewhat analoguous to a sheriff's posse. At the shout of "*Ra mDaa, Ra mDaa!*" echoing throughout the encampment or coming from herders in the pastures, one male from each tent drops all other activity to arm himself and get his horse ready for fast and, if need be, long distance riding. It is amazing how quickly this pursuit posse comes into being—organized, provisioned, responding to orders, and ready for pursuit or rescue.

Once, traveling with two Tibetans, I witnessed a successful raid on an encampment horse herd. Outnumbered and pinned down by gunfire, the three herders were unable to turn back the raiders, but the shooting alerted the encampment and within a few minutes, armed riders were coming out of the winter quarters a mile or so away, in hot pursuit, like angry hornets out of a hornet's nest.

On another occasion in a small encampment a rider arrived just at dusk shouting "*Ra mDaa, Ra mDaa!*" He reported a horse missing. In short time eight armed riders—there were eight tents in the encampment—had gathered, ready to start on an all-night ride. For outnumbered herders, risking all to drive off raiders and save a herd, there is always comforting assurance that, with the sound of shooting, the *Ra mDaa* is gathering and will soon be on its way to rescue or avenge them. Protection of the herds is of prime importance and shared responsibility is as automatic as instinctive reflexes.

Beasts of prey are a lesser but equally constant menace. Wolves are most feared and do greatest damage. Only occasionally do they hunt in packs, but a pair of hungry wolves—nearly white brutes as large as timber wolves—can decimate a flock of sheep and will attack cattle when the latter are weak. In some areas jackals, running in packs, do great damage. They are said to be attracted by the scent of the afterbirth, and particularly attack mares and cows having newly dropped foals or calves. More rarely, snow leopards and lynx take to raiding the herds, and brown bears, newly out of hibernation and hungry, will attack sheep. Against all these predators constant vigilance is the principal defense, and the guardians of the herds always watch for signs of slinking forms that slip along the water courses or pass like pale shadows from hollow to hollow, invisible until the kill has been made.

An attempt is always made to kill these marauders, and, on particularly good horses, there are riders who run down and spear wolves. Trapping is not done and though poison is sometimes used to get winter pelts, its use is frowned on and strictly prohibited in some regions. Nor are dogs used against beasts of prey.

Another aspect of protection is that against insects. In inconvenience, if not actual danger, their menace is very real. Horseflies, gray deerflies, mosquitoes, and gnats can drive herds to frenzy. The stock lose condition, scatter in flight, and sometimes are lost. All the pastoralists can do is to plan successive moves into higher, and then back to lower, country. The life cycle of these pests is extremely short and it too is conditioned by altitude, being later or earlier with each change of only a few hundred feet. It is thus possible to plan the seasonal displacement of the community so that it evades or avoids the insect pest altogether by moving ahead of it into higher country. Complete avoidance of "the time of the bugs" is seldom achieved, but a good pastoralist will take considerable pains to plan movement so as to spare his stock the harassment of the insect plague, or at least shorten its duration. Such effort, too, is part of the protection he owes, if he is to be successful, to his livestock.

Protection of livestock against disease is mostly veterinarian care and the use of remedies, but one aspect of protection against epidemics of rinderpest, hoof-and-mouth disease, animal diptheria, anthrax, and scabies is aggressively protective in nature and requires gathering intelligence and the taking of positive measures to be backed by the threat of force if necessary. The efficacy of quarantine is known, for the Tibetans are well aware of the nature of contagion. The pastoralists take great pains to keep informed about the incidence of cattle disease in nearby areas. To prevent the movement of livestock coming from, or through, areas where such disease is known to exist, strict quarantines are established and are maintained by the use of patrols, guards, and resort to armed force, if necessary. The breaking of quarantine sometimes results in large-scale fighting between communities.

Veterinarian Care

Veterinarian care begins with animal obstetrics—aiding, when necessary, the birth of calves, colts, and lambs—and both men and women acquire whatever skills are needed. Other aspects of medical care, as an essential part of animal husbandry, include treatment of injuries, surgery, the use of herbs, both externally and internally, and the practice of acapuncture* and searing. Broken bones are crudely but effectively set, abcesses lanced, abdominal puncture practiced for bloating and pancreas and liver inflamation, and open wounds treated with hot butter and hot ashes. Infusions made from different herbs are given as medicine, and other substances, such as animal gall, bezoars, and musk, are also used in compounding drenches. One infusion made from herbs and mixed with vegetable oil is very effective in the treatment of scabies. It produces, by shedding and new growth, a drastic replacement of skin within a few days. Grease is treated by wrapping the pasterns in felt and keeping the binding wet with human urine. Acapuncture and searing the skin in selected areas is much used, with some surprising results, for a variety of ailments.

Castrating of bulls, stallions, and rams is a part of herd management analogous to sowing and harvesting in soil fields and will be discussed later in those contexts, but in its techniques and practice it is a part of veterinarian service. It is done quite early—hardly ever later than at the end of the second year—and with a minimum of fuss. In the larger animals, the cut is seared with

---

* Acapuncture is the practice, borrowed from the traditional system of Chinese medicine, of sticking needles into nerve-ganglion areas of the body to produce therapeutic reactions.

a hot searing iron used for a number of therapeutic purposes. It is a short, slightly flattened metal rod made of copper mixed with silver. Iron is not used since it is said to bring injurious heat to the process. With smaller animals the cut is simply smeared with some hot butter. Very seldom is an animal lost because of the operation, which virtually every herdsman can perform.

The great animal epidemics are generally accepted as being beyond medical aid and, as stated previously, quarantine is considered all that can be done. As a certain percentage of the sick animals recover, the principle of immunity is recognized and, in the case of rinderpest, those which have become immune, identified by the fact that the hairs on the tip of the tail are missing, are highly valued. In some nomadic communities I have known of attempts to inoculate cattle to induce a mild form of the disease and produce a reserve of immune cattle to minimize possible losses.

Although in every community it is conceded that certain individuals have special veterinarian knowledge and skills, most herders know most of the prescriptions and treatments used and apply them. This is one more example of the great variety of knowledge and skills which the pastoralist must have to make a living for himself and his family. In the care of his livestock fields, in order to give them guidance in pasturing, protection from animal and human predators, and minimal veterinarian service, he must be, to a successful degree, fighter, hunter, and a doctor of sorts. His subsistence technique, in its variety, is a demanding one.

6

Sowing and Reaping
Livestock Fields

I N PASTORALISM "sowing" and "reaping" are not confined within short periods
of time, nor limited to one season for each, but run together throughout
much of the year. Sowing lasts from early spring until late in the summer
and, sporadically, even later. Reaping is spread over a still longer period, much of it
being done from late winter until late fall, but some continuing all year. Sowing is
not a process initiated by man, but a part of biologic life cycles under limited
human control; reaping, however, requires human skills and tools. Its basic function
is the gathering of subsistence materials and, through surpluses, the accumulation
of wealth. This is aided by a number of subsidiary activities such as hunting,
pursued in somewhat random fashion, but with engagement-satisfaction.

Sowing

Sowing the livestock fields is an essential part of herd management. It requires the maintenance of stud in sufficient numbers and selected quality, and,
in breeding hybrids, it may require human interference. The herdsman does not
arbitrarily initiate the sowing—that results from biologic urge—but he must
know how to create favorable circumstances for breeding with minimum dis-
turbance of the herds and the all-important grazing pattern.

One result of domestication is disruption of the relative breeding-season
regularity found among the untamed herbivores. There is no exclusive period of
rut for the males and, though receptivity of the females to fertilization does have
greatest incidence in certain seasons, breeding does take place with more or less
frequency throughout the year. This state of continuous, but variably low-keyed
rut for the males and a similar pattern of heat for many females creates herd-
management problems. The number of young born in unfavorable conditions—
particularly the bitter cold of midwinter, when the amount and quality of maternal
milk is low—must be kept as small as possible, and this requires keeping stud

animals from brood stock at certain times. Such interference is not easily imple-
mented in the fenceless, stalless pastoralism of Tibet. A pastoralist proverb says:
"They all have four legs." I have seen considerable exasperated riding in the
chasing away of stallions, bulls, and rams.

On the positive side, the pastoralist must plan for opportunity and even
incitement when the time is right so that all ready females are adequately covered,
although repetitive couplings should be avoided, and no pregnancy-and-birth
cycles missed. Planning also involves determination of just which females are
barren so they may be marked for disposal.

The importance of having stud is known and an effort made to select and
keep for stud the best animals available. Little attention is paid to systematic
maintenance of bloodlines, though certain herds in certain localities acquire a
reputation for excellence and attempts are made to acquire individual stud stock
from them.

Yak from high country, where, through contact with wild yak, there is
reputedly more wild blood, are sometimes preferred as stud. Horses from the
horse-breeding districts along the upper courses of the Yellow River are similarly
in demand because of their size and excellence. Otherwise, selection of stud
animals is made on the basis of observable conformation, size, and whatever
promise of spirit and tractability can be determined in the young. The practice of
somewhat early gelding—toward the end of the second season—does not, however,
allow much opportunity for a thorough testing of the capabilities—speed and
stamina, in particular—of any uncut horse or yak. Breeding for excellence in meat,
milk, and wool is mostly a hit-or-miss matter, though certain stud and brood stock
have higher value.

The number of stud animals is kept to a closely estimated minimum.
Frequently, there will be only one mature stallion in an entire community and a
maximum of three or four bulls fit for stud purposes. Because sheep are kept in
greater numbers, rams are more common, but the number of stud stock throughout
is carefully restricted to the requirements of their breeding function, as they are
more or less debarred from other usefulness. Yak bulls are unsatisfactory, and sometimes dangerous, as pack animals. As a half-respectful concession to the maleness
of their stud function, they are not depilated as other yak are. Stallions are noisy,
a nuisance with other horses, and frequently hard to handle; they are to be ridden
only when other mounts are not available. Rams are more numerous, but again are
sheared disadvantageously later than other sheep and, when their stud usefulness is
passed, their meat is inferior. Gelding of stock is done therefore, for a number of
reasons, of which control of breeding is only one. The degree of selection practiced
in that annual routine is an important part of the control which the pastoralist
exercises over the biologic process of seeding his fields.

Breeding for bovine hybrids, an important part of the economy among
some tent communities and tabooed in others, frequently necessitates human inter-
vention. This lends support to the previous suggestion that hybridization was a
purposeful effort to develop an animal which would meet certain needs. Common-
cattle cows sometimes seem unwilling to allow yak bulls to cover and, still more
frequently, yak cows try to avoid common-cattle bulls. In both cases, the women

who can best handle the cows hold and cajole them while the bulls are brought to serve. Such occasions are usually marked, or celebrated, with considerable ribald badinage between the men and women thus involved in pastoral sowing.

Reaping

Reaping, next to pasturing, is the essential subsistence activity of the pastoral economy and also is an important part of herd management. It is acutely responsive to conditions of trade, market supply and demand, and even certain world-wide needs. It is a complex made up of many skills, a variety of techniques, and continuing activity throughout the year. It involves men and women in shared, freely interchangeable, and exclusive roles. These last exhibit polarization of cultural significance marked by taboos, prescribed attitudes, and symbolic artifacts. Reaping consists of: making herd-management decisions as to utilization of the natural increase, milking, shearing, pulling hair, and collecting dung.

Decisions deal with two options. The natural increase may be preserved as a direct increment to the herd. A certain number of newborn calves or lambs are to be held and, in maturity, to develop into milk, wool, and hair resource-production units, thus adding to the pastoralist's fields. Or the natural increase itself or its substitutes—head for head, from the mature and old of the herd—may be either traded for wealth or butchered to furnish meat, animal fat, and skins, which range from the tough hide of an old ox to the tiny pelt of an unborn lamb.

A number of factors affect the choice of options. Immediate need may be pressing, but natural increase inevitably is counterbalanced by natural attrition—there is a death rate as well as a birth rate—and the size of the pastoralist's fields is not unchanging. Natural increase may not be an addition but only a replenishment and, whereas addition may be very much a matter of open choice, replenishment at times is a pressing imperative. There is also the problem of aging. Each animal carries in the condition and number of his teeth an age record showing how much longer his usefulness will last, and when, according to good herd management, he should be disposed of. In the context of production, reaping consists of amassing quantities of milk—and its products—meat, animal fat, hides or skins, hair, the fur of the undercoat and wool, but culturally there is a deep and psychologically painful cleavage between such reaping as milking, shearing, and the taking of hair, which does not involve the taking of life, and that which involves the taking of life for meat and skins. The latter activity is sharply polarized as a male role. It involves the use of the knife and operates within the agonizing dilemma of what in herd management is acceptable, yet in the ethics of Buddhism is not allowable, though—in terms of survival—necessary.

Shortly after the Tibetan New Year's (lunar adjusted to solar), seasonal development of life poses a problem and suggests a reaping, for it is shortly prior to the lambing season and each pregnant ewe carries within herself the much prized pelt called "unborn lamb," the price of which, sensitive to world markets, is a high one. Reaping it requires the taking of two lives, a double violation of the most universally binding law of the Buddhahood. In the context of herd management such reaping also seems a veritable crime against the herd, thus depleted by two in the forfeiture of natural increase for not only one but possibly many years. It is also flagrant waste; meat from the ewe is stringy, a fraction of that of an animal in good condition, and is even considered poisonous by some. The skin is valueless for the making of clothing for the fleece has begun to loosen. The wool may be shaved off, but the skin is not worth tanning.

Many considerations—relative need for immediate gain, size of the flock, prospects of favorable weather to ensure survival of the ewe and lamb in any case, personal piety, a tent wife's emotion-charged preference—influence choice of action. When the decision made is to take the pelt, it is the man—user and wearer of the knife—who does the bloody work, taking life, often with a torrent of prayers on his lips.

Early in spring, the lambs are dropped as the first of the natural annual increases, although the lambs who die from natural causes furnish short-curl lambskins of considerable value. No harvest is taken at this time, but in a bad season these skins may help compensate for weather losses. Lambing time is a period of special activity for the tent wife, for animal obstetrics is a preferred, though not entirely exclusive, female role that gives her an additional emotion-based voice in regard to disposal of stock—young stock in particular. These lambs also furnish scraps of meat, just at the time when the frozen, dried-out meat, stored throughout the winter, is nearing depletion and the relatively meatless season of the year has begun.

Later in the spring the calves of the hybrid cows supply the only veal the pastoralists ever eat. The butchering of the newly dropped calves, always done by the men, though still considered sin, is more acceptable to the pastoralist than any other killing of livestock. The dilemma, whether to keep the animal for trade or as an increment to the herd or whether to sacrifice it, does not arise. If kept alive, it would be of little value and would seriously interfere with the milking. It is maintained, indeed, that the calf must be killed immediately before it has suckled, or the mother will never allow herself to be milked. Veal thus appears like a free gift, and the skins, in desirability, rank with short-fleeced sheepskins for summer clothes.

Throughout this meat-famine period of the year, reaping "live blood" takes place to supplement the diet. Selected cattle—mostly yak oxen and barren cows—are tapped for blood, in considerable quantity, from blood vessels in the neck and shoulders. It is exposed to slow heat in shallow vessels and coagulated into a sort of jelly which, mixed with cheese, is considered a delicacy and is especially nutritious.

In late spring, when shedding begins, reaping of hair takes place. Preference is for pulling the long belly-fringe hair of yak oxen, for only that hair makes the best tent cloth. Stud animals and yak cows with calves are spared the ordeal. The process is not exactly gentle and is men's work, though the women help as needed. The animal is hobbled and thrown. Someone sits on his head to keep him down, and the hair is reaped—but not by shearing, which would result in cut ends and lessen the watertight quality of tent cloth. Depilation is accomplished by wrapping the hair on a thick, round stick, often a heavy whip handle, and literally rolling it off the skin. If the natural loosening of the hair roots preceding shedding is not sufficiently advanced, blood may even seep through the skin in the process. Hair of the tail and the underfur are sheared, as are the belly fringes of hybrids. The manes and tail hair of mares are also sheared, but for appearance sake, the horses used for riding are left untouched.

The sheep are sheared early in summer and sheep's wool is a major crop. Shearing is done by both men and women, using the small, highly sharpened sickle blades used in cutting hay. This reaping—unlike the reaping of meat—is done with no sense of guilt.

Throughout the summer few sheep and, with extremely rare exceptions, no cattle are killed for meat. No Tibetan likes to butcher anything which has not reached peak condition—well-fleshed and fattened. At haying time, some butchering of sheep takes places to supply meat in ample quantity as an inducement to hired labor. The main meat harvest of the year takes place after the return to winter quarters and late enough in the fall so carcasses will freeze, but before sheep and beeves have begun to lose flesh. Selection of the muttons is made from the gelded sheep which are heaviest and oldest. Of the ewes, only the barren are chosen. The beeves are chosen from among the older yak oxen and *mDZo,* those whose teeth suggest that next year they will not be able to put on flesh as well as during the current season. This makes for tough eating, but an occasional barren yak cow will also be butchered to furnish choice, prized meat—juicy, tender and well-marbled.

It is a time of much killing. Even a small tent family butchers as many as fifty sheep and ten or more beeves, for in addition to serving as food for family consumption and in lavish hospitality, mutton and beef are prime gifts. The carcasses are stacked and frozen, slowly drying out in the cold. Such stomachs, sheep or bovine, as are not set aside for use as containers, are filled with viscera—guts, hearts, livers, kidneys, lights, abdominal fat, and the like—and frozen, to be used later in sausagemaking. The skins and hides are dried and stacked. The hair and underfur are scraped from the hides, but the fleece is left on the sheepskins which are to be used in making clothing.

Little of the butchered animal is discarded. Sheep and beef sinew, carefully cut from the legs, is set aside to dry, the heads are stacked for later use, and even the best horns are treasured. The blood, known as "dead blood" to distinguish it from "live blood," is collected for sausage and stews. All butchering is the work of the knife, though actual death is often inflicted by strangulation to avoid the knife's use in the "cutting short of life." Butchering is done only by men, though women help by bringing water for washing guts and taking the hides and skins for stretching and drying. The harvest of meat in the early winter is the last of seasonal reapings in the pastoralist's year. There are, however, three continuous harvests which are year long: milking, gathering and preparation of dung for fuel, and trading, whereby some of the annual increase is changed into value received instead of being kept as accrued increment to herds.

Milking is most in accord with the gentle ethics of Buddhism as applied to a pastoral ideal. It requires no violence, does not depend on the taking of life, and there is no blood. Twinges of conscience over the *theft* of food from lambs

and calves are answered by the comforting assurance that none of them starve. They are only being obliged—in a pattern of universal merit-gaining compassion—to share with other living creatures food that is enough for all. Milking, moreover, directly provides most valued foods—milk, butter, cheese, yogurt, buttermilk, and even whey, which are not only foods but the prestige symbols of pastoralism.

Milking is done exclusively by women. Indeed, cows will not permit an attempt at milking by a man, though most of them will stand without being tied and wait for the mistress of the tent who talks to and caresses them as she begins to milk. Occasionally, a yak cow will try to hold her milk for the calf, but without ado the women, in what looks like a caress, will blow into the vagina of the cow and the milk comes down. Yak cows and the female hybrids supply most of the milk. For buttermaking yak-cow milk, being very rich in butterfat, is preferred, but ewes are also milked during the shorter period when they have milk. The milk pails are small. Milking of both cows and ewes is done with only the first two fingers and the thumb and, at any given time, the actual quantity of milk in evidence—even in a tent that owns hundreds of cattle and thousands of sheep—does not appear to be very great. At the height of the season, however, when milking is done three times a day, the food made available in butter, fresh curds, cheese, yoghurt, buttermilk, and whey is in itself a very well-balanced diet, and stocks of butter and cheese accumulate very fast. The peak of the milking season comes in midsummer, after all the calves have been dropped and while the grazing is at its luxuriant best, but some milking extends into the "starvation time" of late winter and early spring, and the nomad's tea is always white.

In this reaping, an honored one, the exclusive female role unquestionably contributes to the favored position accorded to women. The milking technique itself, in which the pail is held against the right thigh as the woman squats beside the cow with her head pressed against it for balance, has produced a special artifact—strictly functional in origin and use, but become symbolic. Each woman wears, attached to the girdle of her robe and hanging down in front, a sort of double hook of metal, like a flat anchor, which, inserted into a notch in the milk pail, serves to hold it firmly and steadily against the thigh during milking. Often ornamented with silver, coral, and turquoise, according to wealth available—in the same manner and degree that ornamented knives and swords are part of male regalia—these hooks are a prized item in feminine attire. In the context of milk reaping as an essential activity, this hook is the symbolic counterpart of the knife carried and used by the man in his exclusive role as killer and reaper of hides and meat.

Collection and preparation of cattle and sheep droppings for fuel is the most continuous of all harvesting, a daily chore to meet a daily need. Only occasionally does a nomadic community camp near any brushwood—tamarisk, buckthorn, dwarf willow, laurel, and juniper—and as brushwood requires a differently arranged fireplace, it is seldom used, even then, except in emergencies. There are some beds of good quality peat, but its use as fuel is tabooed—the mountain gods and "soil lords" are aroused to wrath by the acrid smoke.

Thus, tent fires, and all other fires, are fueled by dried cow and sheep dung. Sheep dung is best, giving greatest heat in proportion to volume. If bellows are properly used, the ash will clinker, but except in the winter quarters, it is difficult to collect. Cow dung is the fuel most used. In the winter quarters the hard dry-feed droppings quickly desiccate in the dry cold and are easily picked or raked up and stacked or stored in bags. In the summertime, by contrast, the dung is half-liquid and ready to dissolve under rainstorms; it must be prepared and turned into fuel quickly or it will be lost.

Each morning, as soon as the cattle have moved out from the tether lines and night-stand areas, the women collect the wet dung and spread it with their hands in a thin scumlike coating on the grass around the tents. If the day is hot, before noon it will have dried to crust, to be broken up and turned by raking, and by midafternoon it will have become dry fuel to be stored in a corner of the tent. Keeping a reserve of fuel is a woman's responsibility in her role as maker and keeper of the fire, not always an easy task. The balance between sufficient sunshine to turn green dung into fuel and the rains and storms of the season is a precarious one. Every advantage must be taken of breaks in the weather, or the tent may be fireless. This phase of reaping dung is exclusively a female role, but mass collection of fuel in winter quarters may be aided, or done, by men—particularly when it is being collected and packed for sale to the nearest monastery, where it is always in demand as a cash crop.

Trade as Reaping

Trading the annual increase for wealth is the most important reaping of the pastoralist harvest. What proportion of it should be traded is a difficult choice between immediate need and the advantages of long-term investment by allowing crop to become fields. The wealthy, as always, have the advantage. Since they are unpressed by immediate need, they can add steadily to their herds if the problem of herd care *versus* available manpower is not too acute. Those of more modest means must meet immediate needs before adding to the herds. What and how much to reap is also influenced by secondary considerations. A herder, for example, may decide to sell a fat sheep for meat to a passing trader when offered a length of cloth that particularly pleases him, when, prior to that, he had not thought of selling any of his sheep. On a higher level of economic prestige values the owner of thousands of stock may be tempted to trade the good horse he intended to ride for years for a rifle that is the best in his community.

However and whenever a decision is made, the pastoralist operates in a seller's market. On a basic local level meat—an essential food and the luxury half of the national diet—and skins and hides are in demand in the agricultural, monastic, and trader communities of Tibet. Livestock can be moved on their own power to those communities, either by the traders who come to the pastoralist or as he himself drives them in the annual grain-trading expedition. Furthermore, livestock, especially hybrid and yak cows for their milk and yak and hybrid oxen for transport, are the best investment for anyone—farmer, trader, wealthy lama, or businessman monk—who has funds to invest. Cattle and sheep, moreover, move by the thousands to the meat markets of western China. Other traders seek out the best mares, which are sought for mule breeding in China, and the best geldings for the Chinese armies. These are seller's markets for what the herder decides to reap by trading and thus realize as wealth. It brings also the pleasure of bargaining—offer and counteroffer in the best tradition of the market, where gain and loss go together.

Subsidiary Activities

The important subsidiary activities of the nomadic pastoralists—raiding, hunting, and services of transport and escort—are exclusively male roles. They arise out of qualities essential to nomadic pastoralism: wide-ranging mobility; exigency-meeting response and initiative; familiarity with weaponry and the slaughter of animals; reserves of animal power and troil and packer know-how; and an almost instinctive awareness of topography. Other less important activities such as mining, the exploitation of salt and borax deposits, and gathering are less congruous with nomadic pastoralism, but are, nevertheless, techniques for reaping wealth.

Raiding and hunting have much in common. Indeed, a raiding party may turn to hunting, or a hunting party turn to raiding, as opportunity or lack of opportunity develops. According to Buddhist morality, both are forbidden, yet each brings renown, and there is prospect of gain with little investment other than hard riding, strenuous exertion, exposure to the weather, sudden and exciting action, and the forbidden joys of weaponry.

Raiding

Raiding, however, requires acceptance of risk and, with the lurking possibility of death, makes stern demands on courage. Raiding also has extensive sociological ramifications with reference to systems of social control, the maintenance of order within communities, and the ultimate, two-faced, problem of peace and war. Indeed, raiding, as a concomitant of nomadic pastoralism throughout the world, may be considered either a characteristic manifestation of modal personality or a determinant in the creation of that personality.

These same issues will be discussed later in another context. In the frame of reference of reaping, raids are the technique by which wealth, usually livestock, is taken from one community by stealth, the threat of force, or by the employment of force, and transferred to another community. Even when it is stealthy action by a single individual, the community it yet involved; becoming enriched as the individual is enriched. There is also tacit community protection on which the raider may count. Raiding by stealth entails the least risk. If successfully carried out, the identity of the raider is, initially at least, unknown, and anonymity conceals him and his community. Employment of even the threat of force in a raid means identification, and risk is correspondingly increased so that the community, under threat of reprisal and seizure of livestock, lives in an atmosphere of tension and alarms. Employment of force entails the greatest risk of all, particularly if by gunfire, or in hand-to-hand melee, man or beast have been wounded or killed.

There is, indeed, much regret if anyone has been killed in a raid. To the sin of thieving, there has been added the more heinous sin of killing, and the ethics of the Buddha have a strong hold, even on the most reckless. On a more practical level, a blood feud has been started which, unless stopped, may create a chain reaction of reprisal killings. No booty, as chosen cause, is worth such a result. Raiding most frequently takes place from midsummer into midwinter, when the horses are in good condition. Often those who specialize in raiding will try to feed and maintain a horse or two in good condition until late in the spring for the advantage to be had in attack or getaway. Seldom, if ever, do the Tibetan nomadic pastoralists carry out raids against agricultural communities. The practical difficulties for horsemen of the steppe to operate against walled villages and fortlike houses are, in terms of booty, out of all proportion to any possible success.

Most primary raids for loot are carried out against other nomads or, if opportunity affords, and with much less risk, against travelers found in uninhabited country where no one is responsible for their safety. See Ekvall (1952:169–182) for a story of this. Raiding for loot by individuals or small groups is indirectly encouraged because, though the loot belongs to the raiders—carefully prorated— in any final settlement the community as a whole helps in payment of indemnity. Reprisal raids, either for loot or in a blood feud, are mostly on a community level and more elaborately organized than simple robbing raids; raiding may, indeed, rise to the level of warfare.

Hunting

There are many areas in Tibet, even far up in the *aBrog*, that are designated as animal sanctuaries where hunting is prohibited by decree, either because of Buddhistic scruples or because it is considered poaching on the preserves of the mountain gods, some of whom are "gods of the hunt." Nevertheless, in wide areas, still teeming with game, the nomads are enthusiastic hunters. They carry firearms at all times; the demands of pasturing take them close to the haunts of the herbivores of the higher country; they hunt beasts of prey in order to protect their herds, and they are accustomed to taking life for meat and skins. It is most natural to turn to the herds of wild yak, orongo antelope, wild sheep, and gazelle when meat is, or may be, scarce, and to hunt onager, wolf, fox, bear, and lynx for pelts, musk deer for its pods, and stag for antlers in-the-velvet, which bring high prices. Some communities slaughter wild yak for the greater part of their meat for the winter; the wild yak carcasses are stacked into walls within their tents. Some north-plain tent people are half huntsmen, half pastoralist, depending largely on trapping orongo antelope and even killing the *Kyang* (Tibetan onager), which other nomads disdain as food, though they hunt them for their hides. Everywhere wild sheep and gazelle, as opportunity affords, are hunted for their meat and skins. Game animals take on flesh faster in the spring than do domesticated stock and are full fleshed when domesticated sheep are still too thin to be worth the killing. The pastoralist eats their flesh with particular relish for it is both good and does not entail the sacrifice of any animal in his herds. The skin of the gazelle is also valued for the fine soft leather which it makes, and wild sheepskins make superior garments that are particularly warm and pliable.

It is obvious that for the nomadic pastoralist, a good horse between his knees and gun on his back, hunting is exciting pleasure, a heritage from earlier times, when high-pasturage ones were uninhibited by the preachments of Buddhist saints like the eleventh-century poet-saint Mila, one of whose poems tells of converting a huntsman from the killing of a red doe. Very early legends tell in great detail of hunting, equally the sport of kings and beggar outcasts.

Organization of the hunt and distribution of the kill as now practiced would seem to derive from the more formal rituals of a hunting society. All members of the party, even those who stay at the campfire, receive equal shares of the meat. The one who does the actual shooting receives, in addition, the skin and the head, but if he used a borrowed weapon, the owner of the gun gets the head. With game such as fur-bearing animals, a musk-deer buck or an antlered stag, equal division must await conversion into goods or currency. For him who did the shooting, the prestige value of having been successful is, in a tradition that goes back to pre-Buddhist value judgments, a share of greater worth than material gain.

Even one not a member of the hunting party who rides up to help with skinning the game, if he arrives before that is completed, is entitled to a share. See Ekvall (1952:163–166). Once, while hunting pheasants in a valley, a casual passer-by held my horse for me as I beat through the brush. Instead of pheasants, I put up and shot a beautifully furred red fox—it was just the right season late in fall. Because I wanted the pelt for my own use, I was, by custom, under strong obligation to offer him half the estimated price of the pelt, an offer accepted graciously, but as a recognized right.

Miscellaneous Subsidiary Activity

Transportation and escort services which bring wealth in goods and currency flow naturally from nomadic pastoralism. Pastoralism provides ample reserves of animal power—the only power by which commodities are moved across the plateau—and nomadism makes men trail wise and good packers. They are experts at keeping loaded animals in good condition, well-grazed to keep in flesh and with fewest possible sore backs, and moving at their best speed along all trails. They also have well-maintained equipment such as saddles and ropes and know how to saddle and pack. They have been tightening saddle girths and packing loads all their lives. Bad weather and storms in a shelterless land are commonplace to nomads, who, at each halt, make the best of what shelter can be improvised.

Though large, properly maintained caravans are financed and kept by the traders, much transportation from stage to stage is hired from pastoralists along the way, and that hire is paid for in currency or commodities. As harvest of power from pastoral fields, this service is more pastoral reaping than subsidiary activity.

Escort service for both guidance and protection is closely related to transportation and is also casually linked to nomadism. Herding activities, constant seasonal displacement throughout his range, and longer forays in trade and raiding give the nomad not only specific knowledge of trails, fords, and passes but an ingrained sense of topography as well. Slopes are likely to become too steep or drainage contours warn of bogs or impassable fords. Both conditions affect movement in areas where trails are unfamiliar or lacking. The nomad is the ideal guide where road signs do not exist and roads are trails that merge with tracks made by wandering livestock or game. As guide or as one of two guides—for traveling alone is generally avoided—he can set his own fees.

Protection is the other face of the lawlessness and danger, or its threat, that so pervade the thinking of the nomadic pastoralists. The stranger or traveler is, or at least feels, peculiarly vulnerable, and the need of protection may haunt him, or be gently or insistently suggested to him, as he makes his travel plans. Among the mGo Log, for example, the distinction between potential robbers and potential protectors may be blurred and only becomes clear and unequivocal when protection fees are paid. Those tribesmen frequently appear ready—mounted, armed, and blustering—for either role.

Mining and the exploitation of salt fields are less important subsidiary activities and have no real links with nomadic pastoralism. Gold mining, which is exclusively placer mining, is contrary to nomadic prejudice concerning disturbing the soil and robbing the soil lords. It appears to derive from the proximity of historically worked mines, the pressing economic needs of those who live at such altitudes that their pastoralism must be supplemented both by hunting and whatever else gives them some income, and tax policies which require taxes paid in gold dust. This is certainly the case of the people of Mus, south of the gTSang Po river, and of some of the north-plain nomads. A number of pastoral communities prohibit mining altogether and enforce heavy penalties—death, for any unlucky Chinese poacher caught among the mGo Log of the AH Myes Ma CHen region, for example—for any violation.

Exploitation of the salt fields is practiced by those communities who are near, or control access to, the salt lakes of the interior-drainage basins of the central plateau. It may consist of collecting the salt and, for a small fee, packing it in bags for the salt-trade caravans, or it may simply mean levying a small tax on what salt the traders themselves collect and pack. In any case the income is small, but as a result of the association some nomads themselves engage, as prime suppliers, in the salt trade.

Gathering is an exclusively female role, but one of some significance, bringing into the economy both foodstuffs and cash crops. It too is not in accord with the general pattern and mores of nomadic pastoralism, except that mobility somewhat extends the available resources. Gathering is centered on the digging of the minute tubers of the edible potintila, which are found in great quantities an inch or so under the surface in much of the aBrog and are at their best in early fall or just after the ground has thawed in early spring. These Gro Ma have somewhat the taste of sweet potatoes and are regarded throughout Tibet as a delicacy. Though a product of reprehensible digging in the soil, they are "good omen" food and acceptable in religious offerings. They are primarily gathered and dried as supplemental food, but also have good sale value. Another product of gathering is mushrooms, which are found in great quantities throughout the *aBrog*. They are mostly a cash crop. Often called "soil gold," because of color, they are sometimes taboo as food, but when dried, are sold into the China trade for good prices. Other gathering crops include wild garlic and leeks for stews, wild-onion tops for seasoning, and occasional reaping of caraway seed to be used as a supplement, or for flavor, in barley flour.

The persistence of gathering as an exclusively female role in an atypical activity within pastoralism appears to parallel the persistence of hunting as an exclusively male role within the same culture. Both are undoubted survivals from very early subsistence techniques, antedating both agriculturalism and pastoralism, in times when hunting and gathering were the principal means of subsistence.

7

The Harvest

EVALUATION OF THE PASTORALISTS' HARVEST and its uses deals with two categories—those primary materials which, without going through the process of conversion by trade, are directly utilized to meet the basic requirements of human existence: food and drink, shelter and clothing, and fire; and those items of the harvest which are converted into currency or goods in trade and thus supply freely expendable wealth. The two categories are not mutually exclusive. The surpluses of the primary materials used to meet essential needs are mostly either bartered off for other prime commodities—meat for grain, for example—or diverted into the trade category. Currency or goods gained by trading, however, may be used to buy foodstuffs, tent cloth, or textiles for clothing.

Pastoral Harvest and the Supply of Primary Needs

The primary materials which the pastoralist reaps, without being converted to dissimilar commodities, directly meet more of the basic needs of his existence, and supply many more of his wants, than do the harvests reaped by the farmer to meet his basic needs. The skills required in processing the harvests for use, though numerous, are broadly shared by the members of the pastoral community, with comparatively little specialization.

Most of these skills are to be found among the members of a single tent family. Thus, each member comes to have a diversity of skills, some at a craftsmanship level. This, together with the variety of harvested primary materials, gives to the subsistence economy its distinctive autarky: an economic cycle of production, processing, and consumption which, on a basic subsistence level, is largely self-contained and self-sufficient. This, in turn, contributes to the relative independence of the subculture within Tibetan society.

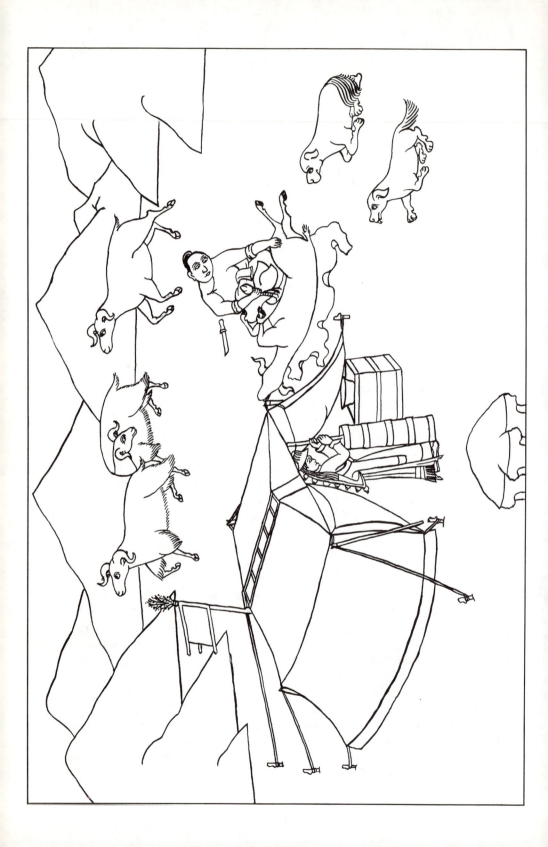

Food

Milk, meat, and blood supply the pastoralists with high-protein components of a diet that is also rich in butter and animal fat. The foodstuffs derived from these three sources are, in themselves, and without additives of fruit, cereals, or vegetables, an amply nutritious diet. Whenever additives are not available, the pastoralists can, and do, live on what their herds supply with greater dietetic variety and richness than a hunting culture could supply.

The daily yield of milk is processed without delay into butter and cheese, although a small portion is kept for making the tea white, for a limited use in boiled form on special occasions, as a drink by itself, and for the day's ration of yoghurt. The milk is poured directly from the pail into the unwashed churn, which contains residues of previous churnings, that hasten curdling, and the churning begins.

There are three varieties of churns: a long, narrow leather bag which is suspended like a hammock to be swung and punched to beat out the butter; one shaped like the leather one, but made of pottery, which is swung and shaken; and a tall, wooden churn with a long-handled dasher which is worked up and down like the plunger in old-fashioned washing of clothes. The leather-bag churn is used in those communities which are farthest from villages, farms, and forests; the pottery churn, said to be a copy of the leather-bag churn, was developed in agricultural communities and is principally used among the *Sa Ma aBrog*. The wooden churn, which is said to be the most efficient for processing large quantities of milk, is found wherever nomadic communities have trade relationships with woodcrafts communities, or wherever there is affluence to pay for the costs of long-distance trade.

Churning completed, the buttermilk is squeezed out by hand and, without further washing, the butter is packed away in sheep stomachs or leather bags. No salt is added, and the butter begins to get rancid very quickly; residual buttermilk in the folds turning green within a few hours and hastening the process. One pat of the day's churning is placed in the butterbox for the day's use; for white tea and new butter are the two favorite boasts of the tent wife when serving guests. Parenthetically, here it should be said that the storied preference of the Tibetans for rancid butter is a story and not a fact. Like anyone with taste buds, they too prefer fresh butter, but there is not much of it, and that little is in the butterboxes of the nomadic pastoralists.

Cheesemaking follows buttermaking. The buttermilk is heated to form curds from which the whey is drained through a haircloth bag. What results, called "wet" cheese, is much like cottage cheese. Some of the daily making is eaten in that state, but most of it is spread out on haircloth in the sun and rubbed into crumbs as fine as possible; when dried it has the feel of coarse sand and can be stored for a season or two. In certain localities whole milk, instead of buttermilk, is used to make a richer cheese; shaped into hard round cakes, with holes in the middle so they can be strung on a cord, this cheese is so hard it must be cooked in stews. Both sheep and yak or *mDZo Mo* milk are usually put together in making butter and cheese, but there is a preference for yak-milk butter and sheep-milk cheese.

Some of the daily yield of milk is immediately warmed and poured into special pails for the making of yoghurt. Even in a poor tent, every effort is made to have yoghurt for at least the evening meal, and tent hospitality is considered poor indeed, if it is not served to guests at any time throughout the day. It has an important place in the Tibetan system of omens, being the most auspicious of all foods and drinks, and is extensively used in religious offerings. Whey, the by-product of cheesemaking, is never wasted. By some, it is considered a good hot-weather drink; by others, a fortifying drink for horses, giving them endurance on fast rides; some is used in the tanning of lambskins; and the tent wife treats the dogs with what remains.

In milking and buttermaking the woman of the tent plays her exclusive, and honored, role as the producer of wealth, which comes out of the churn to pervade the economy and the culture. Butter is an important part of diet (just how it is used will be discussed when pastoralist eating habits and diet are described), and in economics it is the pastoralist's measure, in weight units, of price in the same way that the agriculturalist's measure is weight units of barley. Even when payment is not made in butter, the value of commodities and even currency are quoted in weight units of butter, for example, 2 pounds (Tibetan) of butter for a square of cloth, or 5 pounds of butter for a Chinese silver dollar. It is, indeed, a currency based on its own utilitarian value in the economy. In technology, at its oldest oiliest stage, when no longer acceptable as food, it is the universally used tanning agent for softening all the hides, used in making many artifacts of a pack-and-saddle existence, and for all the sheepskins used for clothing. In social relationships it is the preferred gift in the reciprocal attitudes and responsibilities created by the gift-exchange system; in religious observances, it is the universally preferred offering, because it fuels the millions of butter lamps in Tibetan shrines and temples.

In art, it is the material of which the Butter Image Festival frescoes are made during the New Year's season, thereby contributing to the fostering and perpetuation of artistic skills in every monastery. On yet other levels it is: a universally used cosmetic for protection against the sun, wind, and cold; an important ingredient in a variety of medicinal compounds; and, indeed, in its all-pervasive emanations, persistent and unforgettable, the very odor of Tibet.

Unlike the horse-culture nomadic pastoralists (Mongol, Kazakh, and the like) the Tibetans, with only one known exception, do not milk mares. Among the nomadic pastoralists of Dam, a district three or four days' ride north of Lhasa, mares are milked *by the men* and the milk is used to make kumiss, as among the Mongols. In the seventeenth century these nomads were commissioned by Gushri Khan, the Mongol then ruler of Tibet, to supply him and his court with kumiss, and the custom has persisted to the present; but now, the nomads themselves drink the kumiss and disregard the disapproval of their fellow Tibetans.

The meat and animal-fat harvest, sporadically gathered throughout the year but reaped in greatest volume in the late fall, is the bulk, high-protein, vitamin- and animal-fat-rich foodstuff produced by pastoralism on which the nomad can, if necessary, exist without grain-food supplements. To counteract the possibility of all-lean-meat protein poisoning, the harvest provides fat in abundance, marrow, viscera, and such vitamin-loaded tidbits as the eyes. The men are the killers and reapers, and they also process the harvest. They prepare the carcasses, cut out and roll the sheets of abdominal fat, collect blood, salvage marrow, and clean and otherwise prepare all viscera for storage. Some of the meat is cut especially for drying, but everything else is frozen and stored. Meat is eaten raw, dried, frozen, and boiled—both in stews and as selected cuts—with emphasis on plenty of fat. Most nomads refrain from frying, broiling or roasting, for the odor of scorching animal tissue is believed to anger the mountain gods and soil lords. Actual cooking is mostly done by the women, as tenders of the hearth fire, but the men do most of the cutting up of meat—even when it is minced for various luxury dishes—for the knife again is much in evidence. Meat-harvest activities are male roles and require no skills other than those of butchering, which virtually every pastoralist male possesses.

The milk harvest is reaped and processed by women, and the meat harvest, by men, yet there is a significant age differential in participation. The women fulfill *their* role well into old age, only reluctantly ceding to the younger women. The men tend to relinquish the meat-harvest role with onset of age—more than willing to turn over to younger men as early as possible the guilt-ridden activity of taking life. This may be one of the reasons the women are more prideful in handling the milk pail and churn than the men are in reaping, with rope and knife, the meat from their fields.

Shelter

The harvests of hair and wool are used primarily as raw materials which, using skills broadly distributed throughout the community, the pastoralists transform into shelter for themselves. Hair is spun into thread and woven into cloth with which the "home" tent is made. Wool is made into felt with which shelters are made that may be as diverse as outsize raincoats, supplying a more-than-clothing shelter for a day, or ornate yurts for ceremony, that rank above the black home tent in the way a palace or a temple ranks above a peasant's house. It is, however, the black tent, related in shape and the suspension principle of its support to the classic black tent of the Bedouin—and, in that context, minutely described in the literature (Feilberg 1944:100–104)—which is the home; the shelter around the hearth of the nomadic pastoralists of Tibet.

The tent, typically, is roughly rectangular, having a roof with so little pitch that at a distance or against the skyline it gives the impression of being flat. It varies considerably in size and may be either a rough square or disproportionately long from front to rear. One of average size is 30 feet square and 6 to 7 feet high in the center. The exact proportions vary somewhat according to the cloth used, which may be between 8 and 12 inches wide and is usually woven in lengths of 5–6 fathoms. This length determines the depth of the tent, for the cloth runs from front to rear, but never from side to side.

The average tent is made in two sections, the division running from front to rear, and, as tent cloth is heavy, each section makes a full yak load. The two parts are joined at the front and rear sections of the roof by toggles and loops and at the center section over the hearth are linked by toggle-and-loop cords that form a long, 2-foot-wide skylight and smoke vent. There is also a flap which can be pulled over this vent during rainstorms and snowstorms, and then thick smoke, caught like a dense cloud, must be endured.

When pitched, the tent is supported in the center at the front and rear, to the height of 6 or 7 feet, by two poles. Four short poles prop up the corners, but the suspension that holds the tent taut depends on eight guy ropes, one at each corner and one midway on each side. Each yak-hair guy rope is fastened to the tent roof by a three-cord spread, stretched over the top of a 6-foot external prop pole, and pegged to the ground. The prop poles may be shifted in distance and angle to give any desired pull on the tent roof, which is virtually hung between them. The squat outline of the tent, with guy ropes and prop poles radiating from it, grotesquely suggests some great insect with legs akimbo, like a giant spider in the grass.

The walls of the tent may be stretched slightly outward and pegged to the ground at the bottom, or may hang relatively free like curtains to be raised for coolness and view. There are many regional and individual variations in size, shape, and the like. Some very large tents are made in three or four sections. Others are small and irregular in shape, but all have guy ropes and prop poles. Among tents of the very poor, even the color may be a motley patchwork of haircloth scraps.

Corresponding to the roof, with its dividing line along the smoke vent above the hearth, the space within is divided in two parts. As one comes in through the front entrance by the center pole, on the right-hand side in the far corner is the place for the altar. Prized possessions of the family are stacked along the side. The open space by the hearth is for the men and where guests are entertained. On the left-hand side buttermaking and cheesemaking gear and the kitchen utensils are kept and the women do their work and sit by the fire to eat and drink. In the front corner is the pile of fuel.

Ideally, the cloth for the tent is woven from only black belly-fringe hair of yak steers that has been pulled—not shorn. Spinning is done by both men and women in their spare time, but particularly in the slack winter season, using either spindles or a hand-across-thigh rub that produces very tightly twisted thread. In weaving, done only by women, and in the summertime when the warp can be stretched near the tent, a primitive hand technique is used that, by an over-under shift, gives the product different recto and verso surfaces. Tight pulling and hard pounding of the cross-threads result in a heavy and closely woven cloth, reasonably waterproof when new and becoming increasingly waterproofed with oily cow-dung-smoke soot.

Sewing a tent is man's work, for the stitches must be extremely tight. Making a new tent signals the setting up of a new tent family, for tents are not replaced, but are renewed year by year on a piecemeal basis so that they are never entirely new or entirely old after the initial making. In a well-run tenthold, two lengths of tent cloth are made, or purchased, each year for the renewal of the tent. Each strip is inserted on one of the halves of the tent and next to the smoke vent. This insertion, a gain in roof breadth of about 18 inches, necessitates shifting the roof outward and downward into the walls. From the center outward, the tent is, thus, progressively older and though at the center the cloth is new, black, and tight, at the edges of the walls touching the ground, it is bleached and rotted by sun and rain and in tatters. This renewal, a graduated steady accretion to match a continued sloughing off, is analogous to the renewal of the skin of an organism and gives the home tent a kind of natural agelessness. It is done, by skills common to all, from primary materials reaped from the herds—even the toggles are made of horn—but to set it up, the pastoralist must get tent poles and wooden pegs by trade or by barter. Sheep horns may be substituted for wooden pegs, but in frozen ground, heavy iron pegs are needed, unless boulders are employed as anchors.

Yak hair, of other colors than black, and what is shorn from hides and tails—often adulterated with undercoat fur and wool—is used for making hair rope for tie ropes, hobbles, girths, and packsaddle cruppers. It is also used for weaving medium-quality haircloth for sacking, load covers, saddlebags, and the like. Some of this fabric, considered unfit for making the home tent, is used for making pup-tent-like shelters for those who sleep on the rim of the encampment or where the herds are bedded down. Most pastoral families have one or two smaller tents for travel or picnicking. They may be either a ridge-pole-style tent with rounded ends that requires only uprights and a ridge pole or a rectangular roofed tent, using guy-rope, external-prop suspension.

Some of the wool harvest is made into felt by every family, for there is a constant need and use of felt. It is made during the hot days of summer just after the shearing. Whereas the wool for sale is twisted into loose ropes for baling, with little regard for cleansing or even for keeping it dry (dirt and moisture add to weight), wool used for felting is selected carefully. One kind is made by using fleece just as it is after shearing, without shredding the wool. The entire fleece is pulled and stretched to increase spread and reduce thickness, and is felted without any additional redistribution of the fibers. A very soft felt that is smooth on one side, the sheared side, and shaggy on the other is the result; it is used, principally, for making clothes. Another kind of felt, in great demand for many uses, is made by shredding the wool and spreading it evenly before the felting begins. The actual felting technique is the same for both kinds. The fleece, or shredded wool, is placed on a basketware mat, soaked with hot water, and rolled up in the mat, after which it is rolled back and forth under hand or foot pressure and repeatedly soaked with hot water. Felting takes place very quickly and results in flexible, lightweight material about one-fourth inch thick.

The primary use of felt is to create shelter against rain and cold. The outsized wide-sleeved raincoat made from it is basically a shelter; draped on a man, it looks like a walking tent. When he rides, it covers him, his weapons, saddle gear and saddlebags, and half the horse; when seated at a campfire, it amply shelters him, his belongings, the food he is eating, and, if he so wishes, half the fire on which the food is being cooked; and when he beds down in bivouac, it covers completely his bed and gear. When felt is made into a circular piece, sometimes as much as 10 feet in diameter, it can be used to cover piled-up caravan loads, the traveler, and all his gear, in makeshift-tent style.

From the Mongols, a few Tibetan nomadic pastoralists have borrowed the beehive-shaped felt yurt, but not for ordinary use. The yurt is a much better bad-weather shelter than the black tent, but its cost and weight *versus* shelter area provided, and the longer time required for setting it up and taking it down, are unfavorable factors. Moreover, the Tibetan pastoralists seem to regard the black tent as a part of "Tibetanness" and have stubbornly resisted the yurt for everyday use. Parenthetically, some Mongol tribes in the northeast who have become Tibetanized have changed from the yurt to the black tent as they have changed language from Mongolian to Tibetan and are now known as the *sBa Nag Ba* (black shelter ones). The yurt has, however, been adopted by some Tibetan chiefs to function as the "god house" for the community. Some keep it in reserve for state occasions, or for entertaining high-ranking clergy. Such use of felt is an example of status symbol employment of the wool harvest.

Other uses for felt are numerous and an important part of the material culture. It is employed for lining boots, making hats, lining clothes, making saddle pads and gun covers, for horse blankets, as rugs and extra bedding, and the like. There are so many demands for it within the family or community that it is relatively hard to buy in the open market.

Fire

The harvesting of fuel which meets the essential need for fire has already been described. No processing takes place after that initial gathering, except to keep it as dry as possible during storms, but certain arrangements are necessary for its use. In the oxygen-scarce atmosphere, an open fire requires use of bellows. Some bellows are much like familiar fireplace bellows, but another kind of bellows is a leather bag, usually a goatskin that has been stripped from the carcass without being slit open, having one end open and the other terminating in a metal tube through which draft is forced when the bag is worked or "beaten." Tent fires require only occasional use of bellows to help start them. The hearth is tripod shaped, made of dried clay slabs or long stones plastered with clay, and has a fuel shelf which leads from the rear into the fireplace. The fuel, skillfully fed along this shelf into the fire, burns with a high, blue flame. From time to time the hot coals and ashes are raked from the base of the triangle into the ashpits on both sides to give warmth and to keep the draft open. A well-built fireplace means quick cooking and the glow which warms the tent and makes it the home shelter.

Clothing

Next to the need for shelter and fire is the need for clothes and footwear. The basic garment—of more all-round usefulness than the parka of the Eskimo— is a full-length wrap-around sheepskin coat with shawl collar and long sleeves that is worn fleece in. Basic design is the same for men or women, but differently ornamented. Women wear their coats almost sweeping the ground, whereas men wear theirs hitched up and held by the tight girdle on the hips so that the hem is somewhere between mid-calf and knee length. The fullness of the garment is gathered somewhat higher at the back in folds. The Goloks often wear their coats higher and over sheepskin trousers. Most nomad men only occasionally wear trousers. Women never wear undergarments, except a jacket-shirt, preferably of silk or satin, for gala.

The girdle can be hair rope or leather thong, but every effort is made to have it of coarse silk. When drawn tight around the hips, the man or woman is dressed; when loosened, he stands ready to bed down by falling forward in a curled-up position on the two thicknesses of the coat, the rest of the cloak wrapped around, and the sleeves tucked under his head, a pillow as he sleeps. With girdle pulled tight, the man is dressed for action, his flint-and-steel pouch and his case knife suspended from it, and, most importantly, his sword thrust from right to left under it across the front of his body.

Eight sheepskins make a good-sized coat. For a summer coat, those with fleece an inch long are best, but for the winter, the fleece should be full winter-weight and length—about 6 inches. An eight-skin coat weighs 30 pounds, but when properly worn, with much of the weight carried on the hips, it does not hamper action. The sheepskins are tanned with butter applied as the skins ferment, leather side to leather side, for a few days, after which the stiffness is broken by working the leather against a tanning stick, notched like a saw on the sharpened, inner curve. No lanolin is removed from the fleece, and it soon puts an added protective coat on body skin.

To this basic garment all additions and refinements—lambskin jackets; wine-colored coats of Lhasa woolens, which double as raincoats and hot-weather attire; otter-fur-trimmed moleskin or satin coats to be worn as outer shells; trousers of cotton goods, silk, or corduroy; and satin jacket-shirts for dress—are desired luxury items, but not essential. The skins of the sheep he kills and the manner in which he wears them make it possible for the nomadic pastoralist to live where the temperatures range from $-20°$ to $+60°$ F within a single day. In the hot sun he may ride or walk with his torso bare as his sleeves drag, or are knotted at the waist. With a 20-degree drop, he puts his left arm in its sleeve and hitches the garment higher on his body. Another 20 degrees lower and his right arm goes in the other sleeve and the garment is close around his body; and when temperatures are really low, his collar is over his ears, with half his face shielded by it and whatever hat he may wear, as he nestles in thick fleece 6 inches long, and stays warm.

Footwear and Miscellaneous Items

To match the coat, the other essentials are boots, which are the only footwear. They vary somewhat in design, but basically they consist of a felt-lined leather upper and an outsized moccasin-style leather sole that is unlined. The foot of the boot is then filled with hay, which serves as padding and socks. It is ideal cold-weather footwear, for the hay, which is changed every other day, takes up moisture, gives adequate insulation, yet permits free movement of the nested foot. The top is tied just below the knee with a boot strap. Boot uppers are made from hides, also tanned with butter, which are selected for softness. For the soles, leather from the shoulder of the common-cattle steer is preferred as most durable. Wet-weather boots with thick, hard soles made by bootmakers are trade commodities which wealthier pastoralists wear, but the less wealthy often go barefooted in wet weather to save their boots for the cold weather.

The harvest of hides has many other uses, for example, to make leather bags for storing and packing cheese, grain, flour, and the like, and the indispensable leather ropes used for packing loads. Leather rope is actually a thong about three-fourths of an inch wide and is made in one length up to 6 fathoms, by cutting it concentrically from a single, tanned hide, after which it is again buttered and worked and stretched. Saddle pads are faced with leather and all horse tack, such as bridles, stirrup straps, cinches, and cruppers, are made from it. Replacement demands are high, for wear and tear is great and, in all the exigencies of constant mobility, worn-out equipment is a hazard.

Pastoral Harvest for Trade

The self-sufficiency of the pastoral economy gives it subsistence independence, but does not rule out trade. Indeed, much of the harvest goes into local and export trade. These two trade channels provide cereals, dried fruits, varied foodstuffs, tea, and seasonings to complement, and bring the luxuries of taste into, his diet. They provide the means of ostentation in dress and display, metalware such as kettles and weapons, and a wide range of commodities, including artifacts as common as tent poles, churns, and wooden bowls. They also provide luxury items such as procelain bowls, brocade satin, jewelry, fine rifles, and binoculars.

Trading, mostly by barter for cereals, is the primary concern, but not necessarily of greatest volume or value. Most of it takes place during the yearly grain-trading trip to farming communities and trade centers or markets, and the rest throughout the course of the year as trade caravans and merchants visit the encampments.

On the annual grain-trading expedition, the nomadic pastoralist ventures to travel and trade in the *Rong* (deep valley) among farmers, craftsmen, and shopkeepers. If the market is distant, the round trip may, for some, take over a month, but for others, agricultural communities are only a few days' journey away. It must be after the pastoralists have settled in winter quarters, and also after agricultural harvests have been reaped and threshed so that the farmer knows the extent of his surpluses in grain. It may not be too late, for their stock will have begun to lose flesh, pasturage along the route will be poor, and midwinter ice and snow will have made the trails difficult.

The expedition is a community venture. Each family supplies, if possible, one member to look after the family interest, but a family may commit livestock and animal products to the care of a friend. The caravan is organized in units of six to ten persons—called a "stove part," as they use one fire. Two men can drive, pasture, tether, and load twenty to thirty oxen and take care of other livestock being driven along for sale. The venture is strenuous and demanding and from the community the strongest packers, the toughest bargainers, and those who are cautious yet unafraid are chosen to go. The trip to lower country is relatively easy for much of what is to be traded in on the hoof and easily driven, and the balance—butter, cheese, wool, and the like—has high value *versus* weight, so loads are light. By contrast, the return trip, when the cold has increased, the trail conditions have worsened, and the heavily loaded oxen begin to weaken from hunger and exhaustion, is a stern test for man and beast, and there is much relief when the grain caravan reaches the home encampment.

Seemingly peddling from door to door, or like visitors at a market, the pastoralist yet does business in a sellers' market, for he brings produce much in demand. The farmer holding out for better prices may find that his foot-loose customer has gone on, leaving him with quantities of grain—a product high in weight *versus* value—which he cannot transport to the distant people of the tents. What the pastoralists bring back is principally barley, some wheat and peas, and vegetable oil, as well as churns, pails, and the like, if the farmers are also craftsmen and near forests. If a trade center where a greater variety of commodities are for sale has been visited, tea and luxury foodstuffs—rice, white flour, sugar, red peppers, dried onions, garlic, and spices—will be included in what is brought back. It is the occasion also when the pastoralists stock up on thread, needles, cloth, pots and kettles, hardware, and sundry notions for the year.

The basic cereal is barley, most of which is made into *TSam Ba* (parched-grain flour)—the Tibetan staff of life. It is made by roasting the barley until it pops and then grinding it. Among the nomads this is done in small quantities, for freshness, by hand grinding on querns. Tea, butter, cheese, tsamba, and meat are the main items in the diet. The first four are eaten at every meal, with the possible exception of the late evening one. Before the white tea is poured, small quantities of tsamba and cheese are patted into the bowl just to flavor the tea, and then butter, in quantity depending on appetite and hospitality, is placed in the bowl, and the tea is poured; sometimes salt is added. As the butter melts and spreads on the surface of the tea, some of it is taken up on the fingertips and face and hands are given a protective coating, a pre-meal toilette.

The tea is downed to about the one-third level of the bowl after which more butter, cheese, and tsamba are added and mixed by hand into lumps of brown, oily, cheese-flavored dough, to be eaten either alone or with red-pepper-and-meat sauces or honey. Meat, dried, frozen, boiled, or in sausage form, is served when available and eaten in great quantities.

These foods make up the basic meal at any time of the day or night. Under any circumstances it is a satisfying and balanced ration. The evening meal—an occasion of relaxation and leisure—is quite different. Even in poor tents, some kind of stew—barley grits, meat, and cheese, or other combinations, including potintila tubers—is eaten, followed by bowls of yoghurt. It is also the time when luxury foods—rice, white-flour noodles, or meat and dough combinations like large ravioli—are served on such special occasions as festivals or when guests are being entertained. Always, tea is consumed in enormous quantities and, thus, is an item of trade in constant demand, figuring largely, on an exchange basis, in the wool trade with China.

Of animal-husbandry products, only unborn lambskins are reaped exclusively for the export trade, as other items of the pastoralist harvests, such as butter, livestock, wool, hides, lambskins, and yak tails, are products for which there is a primary demand at home, and only the surpluses are exported. These surpluses, however, may be in great quantity and furnish: livestock to protein-hungry Asian peoples; wool for the carpet factories of the world; and even yak tails to supply beards for Christmas-time Santa Clauses. Special items such as hartshorn and musk—products of a subsidiary hunting technique—also reach outside markets: hartshorn to the apothecary shops of China; and musk to the perfume factories of France. Salt, too, moves into the salt-hungry communities of the southern slopes of the Himalayas; and gathering, as a technique held over from the earliest times, puts mushrooms in Chinese restaurants.

This export trade, particularly in livestock and wool, and supplemented by barter trade with a peasant economy, keeps the economy of the nomadic pastoralists from leveling off at subsistence autarky and contributes to the marked affluence of the society. They are richer than their fellows and in all their boasts and ostentation they show that they know it. Nor do they fear any challenge to their pastoralism monopoly as the high-pasturage ones, for they are rich in the quantity, variety, and value of the harvests which are theirs.

8

Nonmaterial Aspects of Culture

THE ECONOMY of nomadic pastoralism in Tibet thus rests on both material and nonmaterial elements: the former, the resources, primary-subsistence materials, foodstuffs, and artifacts; the latter, the exploitation techniques and routines, and the skills of the culture. Techniques, patterned use of time, and skills are an important part of the cultural heritage, but there are other intangible and nonmaterial aspects of culture that are of very great significance, and they give to the nomadic pastoralists of Tibet, and their culture, distinction as well as distinctiveness. Three of these, because of their primary importance, warrant attention: communication, social interaction and the control of antisocial behavior, and human relationship to the supernatural.

These nonmaterial aspects of the culture must be viewed within the context of their essential "Tibetanness"—Tibetan language, Tibetan social interaction, and Tibetan religion. Yet within this commonality there are important differences in form and function which distinguish the nomadic pastoralist subculture.

Language and Its Uses

Lack of space rules out any extended description of the Tibetan language. That it is distantly related to Chinese, as the first branch off in the Sino-Tibetan family of languages, is generally though not universally accepted by scholars. Certainly, there are many echoes of Chinese root words and basic syntax in Tibetan linguistic usage. That the language is closely related to Burmese is without question. That for several centuries, beginning with the fifth, it was subjected to intensive Sanskritic influence, while the Buddhist religion and syllabaric writing were being borrowed from Indic sources, is indisputable. Even under that pressure, as grammar was distorted to fit Sanskrit paradigms, the vocabulary and colloquial speech showed themselves resistant to outside influence. Loanwords and direct borrowings—even those of religious terminology—were rejected. The native resources of the Tibetan language were stretched and strained to meet a variety of semantic needs. It seems to be a very inhospitable language, arrogantly self-sufficient, but not changeless, and the phonetic refinements of the system, by which it was reduced to writing in the seventh century, have made it possible to gauge with some exactitude the degree of phonetic change which has since taken place.

Rate of change, shown in the pronunciation, has varied according to locality, being more rapid in the center of the culture area and slower in the fringe areas, where pronunciation patterns follow more closely the phonetic transcription dating back over a thousand years.

In northeastern Tibet, a comparison (Ekvall 1939:65–67) of linguistic usage among sedentary agriculturalists and nomadic pastoralists shows that the speech of the latter is more conservative and—in giving phonetic value to letter combinations, prefixes, and terminals—closer to the spelling of the language. Recent contact with nomadic pastoralists from other regions of Tibet (see map) suggests that this conservative tendency—change in each instance being less rapid—has resulted in an identifiable common norm: an authentic *aBrog sKad* (high-pasturage speech) to distinguish it from *Rong sKad* (deep-valley speech) and *Yul sKad* (country speech). Certainly, in working with these informants— and their wives—knowledge of a high-pasturage speech from one area gave greater facility in communication than when dealing with scores of other Tibetans from every part of the land.

This high-pasturage speech appears to be even more inhospitable than current standard Tibetan to loanwords, and to loan ideas, in coining terms for new things or concepts. Standard Tibetan borrows the *idea* of "sky boat" from Persian (via Hindi) for airplane. By contrast, nomadic pastoralists amongst whom I lived borrowed nothing of word or concept. From what they knew of the materials used, and from what resemblance their own experience suggested—as vultures wheel in the sky—they simply called it *lCag Bya* (iron bird). When it dropped bombs, as a Chinese warlord attempted blackmail, bombing became *lCag Gi sGo NGa gZHag* (iron eggs placed). Standard Tibetan has accepted "tank," with only slight phonetic change, as a loanword, but a nomadic pastoralist who learned of Sino-Mongolian warfare had never heard that loanword, so he coined his own contribution to transference of meaning from culture to culture. The tank became a *lCag Gi Glang* (bull of iron) that snorted fire and knocked down and crushed all who opposed.

The speech of the high-pasturage ones not only has precise nomenclature for specifics important in pastoralism—for example, nine words for horse with relation to sex and age and innumerable terms for every color combination—but is image-laden with the excitements of nomadic experience. It bristles with consonants, and *gives*—not lends—itself admirably to storytelling, poetry, and oratory.

A meeting between friends becomes the occasion for orderly chronology of "what has happened since we two last met"? News of the day, distributed by word of mouth, is in careful detail and may include some editorializing. Every episode which, though personal in experience, may be of interest to the community, becomes a story, told with art, which by embellishment and the blessing of time, may become an epic. *aBrog Glu* (high-pasturage songs) tell of pastoral life—attachment to animals of the herd and the joys of horsemanship—or of nomadic adventure—love, hunting, and war. They have a large place in the subculture, and special renown among *all* Tibetans.

Nomadic minstrels include in their repertoires the classic Tibetan epics and stories, but feel free to load them with nomadic and pastoral details and incidents. One *mGo Log* minstrel whom I heard give *Dri Med Kun lDan*, most famous of the Buddha birth stories, with calypso-singer facility, substituted Tibetan pastoral details for Indic ones—yak and their loads for elephants and their trappings—to the great delight of his audience.

It is, however, in oratory—sententious, interlarded with metaphor and aphorisms, yet crisply incisive—that language usage reaches its peak. In the consensus-mediated-and-controlled society of the high-pasturage, achievement of consensus on all levels—from the trivial to issues of life and death—requires oratory and yet more oratory. The talking may go on for days with resort to every device of the art since men first substituted communication for violence and sought to persuade each other.

Social Interaction

Social interaction among the nomadic pastoralists is two-sided: action and reaction, question and answer, consultation and agreement, assignment of role and its acceptance, and proposal of plan and achievement of consensus. There is always the possibility of negative response, but these moves toward unity of purpose and integrated practice deal with every aspect of communal life: family and social relationships, trade and mobility of wealth, coordination of displacement routines, the details of pastoral care, and the exercise of power.

Detailed instances of these aspects cannot be given in a book of this size, but two patterns of social interaction are important for any understanding of how equilibrium is maintained within the society. The institution and ideal of *hospitality* and the mechanisms and pressures of *social control* not only operate within the community but also extend beyond, linking it in social interaction with other communities.

Hospitality

Hospitality is associated with the very concept of classic nomadism—an inseparable part of the "myth of the nomad." In myth-become-reality on the bleak, inhospitable plateau, it is both an institution and an ideal. Within this institution, which not only operates between members of the community—the in-group—but also extends to strangers—the out-group—who associate with the community, there are: roles and accompanying responsibilities, procedures for assuming or assigning benefits distributed among those who participate, and attitudes and traditions which create an ideal that influences behavior and contributes to the culture-ethic.

Two roles, extending hospitality and accepting hospitality, are two sides of a single coin for each person. Roles change according to circumstances, like the coin when it is flipped, and may be subsumed as the host-guest relationship. This relationship answers to some pressing needs within the society. There are no food, drink, and shelter services to be had on a pay basis. There are few, if any, occasions or places where persons may meet to exchange news, discuss affairs, and advertise commodities and prices. There are few possibilities of meeting on an unobligated basis—like the social interaction of loungers in a public square, where there is neither host nor guest. Simply joining a campfire group automatically assigns host and guest roles.

The relationship operates on three levels or, from the standpoint of the host, within three ever-widening concentric circles which, as categories, are not mutually exclusive, but, reasonably clear. Within the innermost circle are the members of his own community, or those of other communities, who knowing him, and being known, feel free to come to his tent on their own initiative. Within the second circle are those, from near and far, whom he would bring to his tent as invited guests on festive occasions. Within the outer circle are all strangers, Tibetans and non-Tibetans alike, who, having been previously introduced or bringing recommendations from mutual friends, come to the tent to establish formally the host-guest relationship.

For strangers, a Tibetan-style introduction is essential. That is much more than mere identification, a casual "this is so-and-so," entailing no more than mutual recognition. By immediately proffering an invitation or by some other social advance each one so identified may move toward the host-guest relationship. The formal, functionally productive introduction is, however, both recommendation and commitment. Those being introduced are recommended to each other in explicit terms describing the standing, character, achievements, trustworthiness, and the like, of each one and telling why, on the word of the introducer, the relationship should be of mutual benefit.

Formal introduction is seldom impromptu, but usually follows some degree of sounding out both parties. Thus, each one will be prepared to present the *KHa bTag* (mouth tied), often called the "scarf of felicity"—a white or light blue scarf of raw silk which is exchanged on formal meetings and accompanies every gift. At this stage gifts may or may not be exchanged, but at some stage the gift is essential and of contractual significance. Its presentation and acceptance symbolize the establishment of obligations and responsibilities by both parties. The one who comes as guest presents the first gift. With acceptance, the receiver assumes the role of host; the giver becoming his protégé. As host and sponsor he is obligated to protect the latter. At some stage of the relationship, he too bestows real or token gifts on his guest, but the value of his gifts is always smaller than the gift he received. When the situation is reversed and he assumes the role of guest, he then gives a gift appropriate in value to his new role.

On whichever of three levels the guest-host relationship is operating, when a guest comes to his host's tent, that coming is reduced to a formal pattern of approach by the dogs of the tent. Every tent has two or three, some have as many as a dozen, large, mastifflike dogs noted for their fierceness. They are "guard dogs," and in that role they exercise control on all—even the most favored and known—who approach. The sign of hospitality is first shown when members of the tent-hold, particularly the women, who have most control over the dogs, rush out to hold off the beasts and escort the visitor to the tent.

There is no casual approach for trivial reasons. Within an encampment, there is no such thing as "just dropping in." In a community where all live in sight of each other, half-in, half-out of their tents with no closed doors or shuttered windows, visiting for trivial reasons is at a minimum because the dogs establish a zone of danger around each tent and create needed social distance. Visiting is not casual.

Whether the visitor is from the immediate community, is a guest specially invited to a festive occasion, or is a stranger from a distance, his reception is essentially the same. Having been escorted through the dogs, he dismounts at the tent door. His horse is then taken for hobbling, his saddlebags and raincoat are taken from the saddle, and, meeting a chorus of welcome, he enters the tent. In Tibetan good manners he is careful to take his gun from his back and his sword in its sheath from his girdle and lay them aside where the weapons of the tent are kept. He presents his gift, holding it in both hands with the scarf of felicity spread over it. Received with studied nonchalance, it will be exhibited in a place of honor for the rest of the day. He is then shown to a rug by the fire and the best the tent possesses—white tea, butter, cheese, tsamba, boiled meat, and yoghurt—will be served. If it is festival time, there will be such delicacies as meat cakes, dumplings, and sausages and the like.

Lavish entertainment, to the point of straining of the tent resources, is in high-pasturage tradition where invitations are coupled with boastful assurances that there is an abundance of butter and meat. There is a story in Tibetan history of a high-pasturage one of the eleventh century who invited one of the renowned saints of the time in somewhat less than completely respectful terms: "When you come to the high pasturage, you will have a *good* horse on which to ride, there is *plenty* of butter and milk and as to meat, when you people entertain, you cut a small bird in four pieces, but we butcher a young yak." He was, nevertheless, a devout disciple and the saint did visit him with recorded profit.

Hospitality surrounds the guest with good cheer and the comforting assurance that he is among friends while attention is given to the reasons, as he states them, for his visit. If a trader—coming ahead of his caravan to make necessary arrangements—he will be shown where to place his camp near his host's tent. After his camp is made, fuel, water, and milk will be brought and, with the building of his own campfire, his life in the shadow of his host's tent begins. He has, indeed, become someone who is "owned" by his host as sponsor and protector. Protection within the community, guidance and help in trading operations, assistance in making arrangements for the care of caravan animals, and assurance that in no way will he be subjected to harassment, all flow from the "bDag Po" (owner) to his guest and, ideally, should meet his every need. Whenever challenged, he simply refers, or appeals, to his host. The latter is obligated to give protection in a society where there are no police, no insurance agencies, and a high level of hazard in everyday living. The host will also introduce his guest to friends in nearby communities, who thus become hosts-to-be.

Throughout his stay, a continuing exchange of small favors goes on between the guest and his host. When the guest leaves, depending on the warmth and understanding established between the two, the host will either assume responsibility for escorting him to the next community where he already has a sponsor, or by introduction can be passed on to one, or will help him hire escort service. If the host himself goes as escort, he may accept hire, but the tradition of hospitality at its best is to guide and protect his guest without pay.

In the first stage of this relationship, envisaged as a pattern of continuing social interaction, the host receives greatest material benefit, but his is the heavier responsibility. He is committed to taking strong initiatives and accepting appreciable risks on behalf of his guest. He is under social pressure to be the ideal host, and if he does not succeed, his prestige will suffer. Fewer and fewer will be those who ride to within hailing distance of his tent, calling his name as their *bDag Po* (owner) and seeking safe conduct through the dogs so they may sit by his fire as guests. Departing guests, beholden to him though they may be, are also potential hosts on whom he, in turn, may call for hospitality and all it includes when roles are reversed and he is a stranger in a community other than his own.

In the highly mobile life of the nomadic pastoralist, the reversible host-guest relationship is an important web of social interaction which provides insurance to cover the exigencies of travel, guarantees sponsorship, recognizes position, protects against harassment within a community, and gives status and prestige to a man. The larger the host-guest web and the more numerous its strands—linking individuals in genuinely warm interpersonal relationships—the greater is a man's power and importance within his own society.

Social Control

There are three levels of social interaction within a community: (a) that between individuals as individuals, their own concern and nobody else's business; (b) that in which the community is involved as a shadowy presence looming behind the individual protagonists and making them feel the weight of community consensus; and (c) that of the individual *versus* the community. The offer and counteroffer of price in trading is a good example of the first level because, unless friction develops, the community cares little whether agreement is reached or not, and certainly will not exert pressure. Discussion of how to pool manpower in care of stock, which takes place in the context of strong community consensus that agreement should be reached, is an example of the second level for, at whatever of these two levels interaction takes place, there exists the possibility that it will be blocked or compromised by antisocial attitudes or action. This situation leads to the third level of interaction, where the contest of wills and interests is between the individual and the community.

Among the nomadic pastoralists this contest is exacerbated by a number of factors. The high-risk emergency life which they lead places premiums on aggressive personal decision making, quick and drastic response to exigencies, and willingness to take calculated risks. The same qualities carried over into social interaction and, particularly, into the confrontation of the individual with his community foster antisocial attitudes and raise the frequency and level of antisocial acts. In all interaction, individuals loom large—one against another—or to challenge the will of the community.

To modify antisocial attitudes and forestall antisocial acts, emphasis is placed on the ideal of harmony. The aim is not to "keep peace"—peace, like war, is an intercommunity concern—but to "preserve harmony." Disharmony threatens the nomadic community with fragmentation more, perhaps, than other communities, and the will to survive makes the community sensitive to discord within itself. When disagreement festers into rancor and overt ill will, there is danger, for, given the nomadic-pastoralist personality, attitudes change and move into action suddenly and fast. Much effort in persuasion, mediation, and the good offices of mutual friends is devoted to assuaging hard feelings and satisfying personal preferences in matters of communal concern, in the attempt to keep antisocial attitudes from developing into antisocial actions.

When antisocial action threatens, the social control mechanism is brought into play to accomplish what in our society is sometimes called "binding persons over to keep the peace," or to invoke the sterner measures of law enforcement with penalties. Though having similar objectives, what does take place among the nomadic pastoralists of Tibet is scarcely recognizable as the same thing. Binding persons over to keep the peace becomes tying the affair by mediation and consent of the parties; law is not a code which may be violated but guidelines for arriving at a settlement; enforcement is not judgments and verdicts, but achievement of agreement by mediation; and penalties become negotiated indemnification and fines rather than punishments.

Tibetan law as such is a composite of the following elements: concepts from very early times when direct, first-person reprisal and the fear of such reprisal constituted the only devices of social control; folk law, which is custom, and usage which developed as communal interest and consensus modified reprisal by substituting restitution and fixed—and accepted—indemnification; royal law, promulgated by early kings as rules of public order for their expanding empire, and successively revised and codified into national law; and canon law from which such rules of Buddhist monasticism as appear applicable may be adapted to the needs of society. This amalgam, strongly permeated with the ideals of the Buddhist ethic, is the law of Tibet.

There is no distinctive "law of the nomads." In principle, the law of the land applies to them as to all others, but its application is affected by their character and their way of living. Recourse to reprisal is commonplace. Folk law is more frequently invoked than royal law, for pastoralism, with its more fluid wealth, favors indemnification, and custom is stronger than codes. Royal law is weakened, for nomadism interposes distance and relative inaccessibility against the reach of the "long arm" of the law. Canon law becomes a part of the religious dilemma of the pastoralists, wherein the stock-butchering, meat-eating, skin-wearing reality of pastoral life must make its peace with ideals of nonkilling that were born within a grain-harvesting, fruit-gathering, vegetarian, cotton-wearing way of life.

Enforcement of law follows the principle that antisocial acts such as sheep or wife stealing, or setting fire to pasturage, or the pollution of springs are offenses against individuals or the community rather than violations of a code. That stealing is morally wrong is recognized, and often well preached, but the problem of theft remains.

The mobility of pastoral wealth—fields and harvests are all on the hoof—makes it temptingly easy to drive off wandering stock or, by quick action, to convert stray sheep into meat for the pot and an unidentifiable skin in a saddlebag. If community harmony is to be preserved, the problem is to get the sheep back to the owner or, if that is impossible, to put enough pressure on the thief so that he will indemnify the owner sufficiently so that the latter becomes willing to call quits in the matter and not himself take action in reprisal, thereby starting a chain reaction of possibly unending violence and counterviolence to threaten community harmony. Though the matter at issue is basically between individuals—owner and thief—the community is also involved. Community consensus is well aware that stealing is antisocial, but is also colored by the feeling that in case of real need such as actual destitution and hunger the act has some justification—life being more important than wealth.

In the interest of harmony the community, through its leaders and acceptable go-betweens, takes action: (a) to seal off reprisal and violence by securing a pause, or cooling-off period; (b) to mediate and secure agreement on the giving and accepting of indemnification as a substitute for reprisal; (c) to secure agreement on the amount of the indemnity; (d) to bind the parties to keeping whatever agreement is reached; and (e) to supervise and validate the payment of indemnity.

This in general is both principle and procedure in the exercise of social control. The principle is adhered to throughout, but depending on the relative gravity or the particular circumstances of the case, procedures vary. In minor matters, such as verbal vilification, all the steps may be compressed into one continuous operation, wherein agreement is reached and indemnification is carried out. In homicide, as the offense of utmost gravity, each step, however, becomes a complicated operation requiring much effort on the part of mediators, playing quasi-professional roles, and possibly months of time. See Ekvall (1954a) for more details about homicide.

Paying indemnity is not the same as making a one-for-one restitution. In the case of theft, for example, acceptable indemnity is greater in value than simple restitution. This differential may vary, according to the relative statuses of owner and thief. Indemnity paid to a chief or high ecclesiastic may be fixed at from threefold to ninefold the value of what was stolen. Even when such considerations do not enter into the case, at least some percentage of value is added to the indemnity as a token of apology to the injured party and to the community. Indemnification for personal affront or injury, for example, is chiefly or entirely token apology, expressed in value payments, not in restitution. In the remembered and frequently cited customs of folk law, and in the codes of royal law, scales of indemnification for all offenses against individuals or the community are quite well standardized and have the weight of precedent, if not sovereign law, to guide the mediators and pressure the parties toward agreement. Of more immediate importance is what constraints and pressures bear, or can be brought to bear, on the parties concerned to lead or impel them toward agreement. Chief of these is the fear of reprisal. One who fears can never know when or in just what form reprisal may take place and the threat and uncertainty haunt and hamper his every activity. He is a prisoner of his fears. The one who holds the initiative, however, can never be certain to what degree of escalation reprisal may lead—outright seizure of wealth, leading to personal confrontation, with violence leading, possibly, to homicide—as each degree threatens ever intensified counterreprisal. In addition to the argument, cajoling, and implied threat the mediators bring to bear, community consensus, despite some partisanship, is for agreement and against disruption and fragmentation of the society and, in the "little community" of the encampment, can make itself strongly felt.

The men called "between reconciliators" and "straightforward witnesses," who assume the role of mediators, are key figures in this system of social control. To qualify for the role, and to be successful in it, they must be persons of standing with reputations for fairness and able to argue like lawyers. In prestige and ability they must be characterized by what the Tibetans term "mouth-face." They fulfill the dual role of judge and jury, though they render no verdict and pass no judgment. Their function is to find a level of indemnification which, by persuasion, argument, and a certain amount of coercion by implication, can be made acceptable to both the one who pays and the one who receives payment. Their announcement of this judgment by mediation, duly ratified by the voiced agreement of both parties, is the goal and climax of the judicial process by mediation.

At any stage of the process each of the protagonists has the right to veto agreement. Unless he has enough justification to win strong partisan support from the community, however, withholding agreement may set him at odds with community consensus and he may find himself under heavy pressure. It then becomes a contest of interests and wills between the community and the individual. In this contest the individual, because of his own mobility and the mobility of his dwelling, his fields, and all his wealth, has a relatively strong position. Whenever community pressure becomes unacceptable, he has the capability of withdrawal from that community and he need not leave anything behind him in pawn. He is uniquely foot-loose and not inexorably bound within an unacceptable situation.

Withdrawal may be temporary—indeed, antisocial action may be followed by immediate flight or a shift to a neighboring community pending settlement of the matter—or it may be prolonged and even permanent. It may take the form of a protest, without an outright break, by announcing a decision to go on pilgrimage, which is impeccably religious, sanctioned by public opinion, and quite safe from hindrance. For nomadic pastoralists pilgrimage often involves movement of the complete tenthold, with the bulk of the livestock in long wandering with many detours and stops wherever there is grass for the herds. A family may be gone for one to three years, yet it is pilgrimage, though there may be uncertainty as to whether the tenthold will return to the community. Generally, there is more high pasturage than there are pastoralists to occupy it, and among most of those communities "population hunger" assures a welcome.

Withdrawal can also take the form of a sudden break, carried out at times of confusion, as when all are moving to fresh pastures and the community is too preoccupied to interpose effective hindrance. Such flight signals the will to defy community consensus and continue the contest with increased intensity. It is in the interest of the community to block it if possible or, at least, to retain control of the livestock as leverage in continuing the pressure toward agreement. There is added menace in such withdrawal, for feuding between communities, or tribes, is very common. The warmest welcome to a rebel is in an enemy community where, because of his special knowledge of terrain, routines, and the like, he is particularly dangerous to the society from which he broke away. This fact, clearly recognized by everyone, also strengthens the individual in his resistance to communal pressure.

When antisocial attitudes and actions extend beyond the society and develop into intercommunal strife, it is the community that makes war; waged, however, to secure advantages in the seizure of stock or hostages rather than to inflict outright defeat. The nomadic pastoralists are well-fitted for such warfare for their habits, the exigencies of their subsistence technique, and their whole pattern of life is an effective training in the essentials of warfare. See Ekvall (1961c:1250–1263) for detailed elaboration of this theme.

Development of this strife situation *between* communities follows the general pattern of similar development *within* a community. Antisocial action immediately produces the threat of reprisal. The situation then is recognized as a menace to peace—possibly already a form of warfare. In time, mediators seek to secure a truce or a freezing of the situation and mediation is then continued, until agreement is reached and peace is made or until mediation breaks down and strife reasserts itself. There are, however, two differences that are of importance: A basic change in the relationship of the individual to his community takes place; and each aspect of the affair becomes blown up and enlarged.

The change of relationship follows interaction as the individual seeks community protection and backing against enemy individuals involved in the initial confrontation. They soon lose their identity, however, and merge with their own community to become the corporate enemy. In exchange for backing and the assurance of group solidarity, the individual inevitably turns over the power of initiative to the community and its interests become paramount. The community as a whole, operating through traditional procedures for achieving consensus, decides whether or not to undertake a raid and, if so, when and how, whether to give assent to tying of the affair—thus becoming committed to a truce; whether to agree to mediation and the credentials and acceptability of the mediators; and whether to accept the results of mediation and be committed to their implementation.

Enlargement is the inevitable accompaniment of all corporate undertakings. The "between conciliators" are no longer two or three respected neighbors getting together with little fuss and going about the business of mediating, but must be important men from other polities—chiefs, famous lamas, noted orators, and men of affairs—who can only meet in competitive ostentation after considerable delay. They bring weight, but also tedious slowness, to all proceedings. They must be fed and entertained. They are in no hurry to go home for they have oratorical reputations to maintain. They talk about indemnification on a scale grand enough to warrant fulsome citations and endless argument. They are gathered to discuss not a feud between individuals but war between polities. They are weighted down with the responsibility of bringing peace to communities who see themselves as, and behave like, miniature states. See Ekvall (1964b:1119–1148) for other details concerning the making of war and the making of peace among the nomadic pastoralists.

Religion

That form of Mahayana Buddhism known as Tibetan Buddhism is for all Tibetans, with a few minor exceptions, the framework within which their relationship with the supernatural operates. It is a composite of abstruse philosophy, formalized doctrine, and an extensive pantheon. As philosophy it is profoundly concerned with the nature of existence and the nature of knowledge. Such considerations as the relation of "being" to the "void," and such concepts as that all existence is on three levels, the absolute, the relative, and the illusory, have developed.

Doctrine defines the focus of worship and enunciates moral principles, monastic rules, and guidance in tantric exploration of, and experimentation with, the psyche. Worship focuses on the concept of *dKon mCHog gSum* (Rare-Perfect-Three), also called "the Jewel Triad"—consisting of the Buddhahood, the Law, and the Community—which in function, if not in being, is analogous to God. Compassion toward "all sentient beings" is basic morality and from it stem all the virtues. Monastic rules—primarily for "the community" but, as guidelines, valid for all—are directions on conduct and avoidances in the individual's progress toward final liberation in nirvana, as life and death take him through the cycles of rebirth, and rebirths are determined by *Las* (works), or karma, of previous existence. Tantric guidance in psychic experience seeks to help individual progress toward realization and enlightenment, but may become a search for magical powers, following the example of the great tantrist Padma Sambhava.

The pantheon seems virtually limitless: Buddhas and Bodhisattvas perpetually releasing emanations, borrowings from the Hindu pantheon of numerous gods and demons, and the even more numerous spirit beings of every category taken over from the earlier pre-Buddhist folk religion of Tibet. Among those of the latter class there is a continuing, perceptible, increase. In the goblin class, for example, ghosts of the newly dead, having strayed from the round of rebirth, become additions to the fluctuating population. Gods also may have two aspects, the wrathful—which has given rise to some terrifying iconography—and the mild.

To these concepts of the supernatural and its myriad denizens, the Tibetans respond with a depth of devotion, shown in allocation of effort, time, and wealth, that has made Tibetan society and culture the classic example of religion-oriented living. The response is conciously based on the attitude of faith, which means acceptance of the Buddhist postulates of being and of the supernatural, and is expressed in four principal "religion-works" (that is, observances and their combinations), to which Tibetans devote a great amount of effort and time—often to virtual exclusion of other concerns.

The primary observance is "mouth pronounce" (that is, verbalization), which means praying, called "sowing of wish ways and petitions," and also its activation by such devices as prayer flags and prayer wheels. Emphasis is on repetition, which suggests that word magic is an underlying principle by which the word becomes identified with the concept it represents, so that sounding the word activates the concept. Thus, speech is devoted to interaction with the supernatural and the prayer word is sown to produce, of itself, harvest result. Material possessions are made productive in the realm of the supernatural by "offerings" that range from the flipping of a pinch of tsamba to the spirits at the beginning of a meal to donations on a grand scale to build a temple or support a monastery. When the giving up of a son and personal renunciation are combined with large-scale endowments, the offering produces the monastic community, the third, in addition to the agricultural and pastoral communities, of the subcultures of Tibetan society. Physical effort is directed toward the supernatural in "hand beseech," which is the making of salutations that includes hand poses and gestures and strenuous forms of prostration. The "round," that is the performance of circumambulation, clockwise circling of an object of worship, is also physical effort and follows the solar and cosmic pattern in the northern hemisphere. It is suggestive of uncounted cycles of change leading to eventual nirvana.

These forms of approach to the supernatural are found in most rituals of worship, but particularly in two kinds of pilgrimage, short ones to nearby shrines, and long ones, which may last for years, as holy places within and outside Tibet are visited. To this religious travel Tibetans devote an incalculable amount of effort, time, and wealth.

What has been said thus far applies to all Tibetans, agricultural as well as pastoral, but there are appreciable differences, in attitude and emphasis, in the approach of the nomadic pastoralists to the supernatural.

Insofar as the pastoralists are conservative—more inclined, for example, to the old savage practices of the hunt—they display leanings toward the early folk religion of the land. The mountain gods of the past—superficially "converted" to Buddhism—are closer to them in both geography and in sensed presence. The pastoralists' movements in the high pasturage take them to and around such great peaks as gNYan CHen THang lHa, (argali-great-epic-god), where every name points back to worship of the most ancient of gods. The nomadic pastoralists are not only conscious of the constant scrutiny of the mountain gods but when they go hunting, which they do more frequently than other Tibetans, they engage in folk-religion rituals and shout demands to those gods for bloody success, in terms of many killed or big heads, while they promise even their weapons a taste of blood.

This leaning, and the unescapable consequences of pastoralism, involving a close-at-home, constant, calculated taking of life in order to exist, sharpen the contradiction between what the nomads must do and what their creed would have them not do. The Buddhistic creed, developed in a grain-harvesting, fruit-gathering culture by those who wore cotton, has no place for the killing of animals for clothing and tolerates only a degree of evasiveness for the killing of animals for food. But the nomadic pastoralists cannot evade the issue. They must have meat, and as even wool fabrics are not protection enough against the cold and blizzards they have to weather, they must have sheepskins.

To what degree this dilemma, and the guilt that follows, condition the response of the nomadic pastoralists to the prohibitions and promises of his creed is difficult to gauge. By what criteria can degree of faith and intensity of observance be measured? The externals are observable, but the inner flow of psychic participation eludes definition.

Possibly, it is because pastoral routines furnish opportunity for combining watchfulness with praying, when guarding the herds or riding on patrol, that verbalization, with beads to keep a tally, or the spinning prayer wheel, does seem such a part of the herders' life. Maybe it is merely a spin off from affluence that makes offerings, and most generous ones, so much a part of pastoralism that when a lama travels through the high pasturage, his attendants fan out to every tent, where the tent wives are more than ready to put pats of the day's making of butter and outpourings of cheese into the proffered leather bags. Reports by lamas of the offerings they have received when traveling among the high-pasturage ones often itemize hundreds of cattle and sheep. One monk informant told me of seeing a wealthy man of the tents divide his herds, head by head, into two halves and give one of them to the lama of his preference. Whenever a monastic institution is in special need of funds, the first reaction of the management is to plan a tour of the encampments with which it has sponsor-client relationships.

Because nomadism appears to require a fixed point of reference, the nomadic pastoralists have a special relationship with the monasteries within or nearest to their range. For all Tibetans a monastery is a place of worship, a museum of their culture, a place where arts and drama flourish, where their sons, brothers, and nephews are devoting lives to religious research and advancement, and where the stored-up learning of the centuries is being handed down in teaching. It is a place in the vicinity of which trade takes place and where social interaction of every kind is intensified and broadened.

To the nomads, moreover, it is also a place where they may store valuables and other belongings with some relative monk who has a safe space between walls, and within doors which can be locked. In the spring they bring winter clothing and gear, surplus stocks of food, unsold bales of wool and skins, and the like, to the nearest monastery so that they may be less hampered during summer and fall moves, and after their return to winter quarters they take their belongings out of storage in the monastery. It is also neutral ground where intercommunity communication can best take place. The *mTHaa Ba* (the edge), the trade-crafts-services lay community that is a part of every monastery center, is where trade can be carried on to good advantage and where the nomads can command the services of craftsmen to supply a variety of artifacts.

It is religion, however, in its manifestations and proffered opportunities, which exerts the strongest centripetal attraction on the pastoralists and like a magnet draws them to the monasteries in vast numbers for purposeful and prolonged stay. The great festivals are drama, crowd excitement for those who have been alone so much, and occasions when the pastoralist too is treated handsomely as a generous supporter of the establishment. But transcending all material and secular considerations, they are times of blessing and, in wonder and worship, of interaction with the supernatural. In all this mixed involvement of the sacred and the secular it is impossible to say that the nomadic pastoralists are more purely pious than other Tibetans, but the net result is that they bring not only added wealth but also amplified participation and presence and deep devotion to the support of the monasteries. See Ekvall (1952:79–90) and (1964c:283–296) for illustrative material on this subject.

Divination and its place in nomadic pastoralism are also a part of inter-action with the supernatural. Though its position in formalized religion is question-able, its relation to the supernatural is indisputable. It represents the attempt to tap extrasensory and extrahuman sources of knowledge and, by bridging distance and telescoping time, to bring them into the here and now as an aid in decision making, for so little is known about so many matters. There are no weather reports to forecast storms, or heavy snow, no market reports to show price trends in wool, no road reports to give trail conditions and tell whether passes are blocked or streams are in spate, no news media to tell of political, economic, and community events and change. Yet the need for such information in planning pastoral care, trade ventures and schedules of movement is acute. In divination the search for guidance reaches into the supernatural by employment of mechanical applications of chance such as counting beads, throwing dice, and scattering pebbles on marked boards. Mixed subjective-objective omen divination is also used, as in interpreta-tion of smoke from fires, of the calls of certain birds, of dreams, and the like. Direct appeal to deities for answers through those who, as the "god-seized" or "god-ridden" ones, speak from out of trances and seizures with the voice of the god, provides further aid in decision making.

In their search for guidance the nomadic pastoralists constantly resort to divination, but not without some skepticism, which, nevertheless, does not keep them from resorting to it again and again. The majority of those who practice divination are lamas, which lends religious authority to what they say, but they are also men who have access to more information than their clients, which often gives a shrewd hard-headed quality to their advice. Divination does help: by making the individual feel that decision making is being shared; by causing him to examine logically his problem in putting his question; and by giving him, once a decision has been made, doubled assurance in action, for in his world view he has been in touch with the supernatural. See Ekvall (1963a:31–39) for more details about divination.

9

Character Traits and Modal Personality

IN THE SEARCH for an explanation of the dynamics of nomadic pastoralism, attention has been focused on kinship patterns, social structure, need for wide pastures, and the like, but it is the individual who is the pivotal center of dynamic interplay. His character—the norm of his reaction to stimuli—is of primary importance. He is the one who acts, and how he acts is, in part, a function of his personality. In this description of the nomadic pastoralists of Tibet it is not the personality of one specific individual which is of prime value, but rather a species of construct personality that reflects behavior norms of a majority of the members of the community and which helps us understand the people, their culture, and their dynamic interaction. This construct is called "basic personality," or "modal personality."

Unfortunately, there are no data, gathered by scientific techniques, on the personality of the nomadic pastoralists of Tibet. There are available, however, informal character assessments made by those who know the high-pasturage ones. As a check on these impressionistic judgments, what is known about the personality determinants—childhood, experiential, situational, and ethos-cultural—operating in their way of life can be examined for whatever causal corroboration they may furnish.

Personality Traits

A list of personality traits bears much the same relationship to modal personality that a list of the bones of the body bears to a life-size full-length portrait. Both list and portrait, yet ever remain at one remove from the living reality. Character traits, however, are basic, just as some artists insist that "the bones" underlie, or are within, the portrait.

The personality traits listed by Westerners, such as missionaries and travelers, reflect the varied and frequently contradictory circumstances under which they were in contact with the high-pasturage ones, who are called hardy, cheerful, bold, friendly, unfriendly, generous, rapacious, hospitable, burly, surly, swaggering, suspicious, and shy. The Chinese-Moslem traders, whose long-range ventures among the "people of the black tents" give them ample opportunity to form judgments and who also depend, in some degree, on the correctness of such estimates of character, call them brave, enduring, naively honest, forthright, hospitable, trustworthy, energetic, loyal, fierce, truculent, and dour. Other Tibetans, farmers and traders, call them lavish, terrific, fierce, able, unafraid, brusque, straightforward, simple, and proud. The pastoralists arrogate to themselves general superiority over the agriculturalists; are conscious of freedom, and correspondingly free in action; boast of their own hospitality; and are unabashedly proud—with a pride never more aptly defined than in the Tibetan term *NGa rGyal* (I win).

From my own experience among them I can strongly endorse the definitive configuration of modal personality which emerges when these lists are put together and would also like to cite what Dr. Goldschmidt (Goldschmidt 1964:405) writes about African pastoralists (who are not nomadic at that).

> "The personality attributes of the ideal pastoralist may be summarized as follows: a high degree of independence for action; a willingness to take chances; a readiness to act, and a capacity for action, self-containment and control, especially in the face of danger; bravery, fortitude and the ability to withstand pain and hardship; arrogance, sexuality, and a realistic appraisal of the world."

Of the same people Dr. Edgerton (Edgerton 1964:446), after using some current personality-assessment techniques to study the difference between farmers and herders, says, in summary, of the latter, "The herders, on the contrary, are direct, open, bound to reality, and their emotions, though constricted, are under control." This is said of pastoralists who are not nomadic and, as indicated in the section on social interaction, the mobility of the true nomads heightens the sense of freedom and tends to accentuate these qualities.

Personality Determinants

It is generally accepted that behavior patterns are transmitted, and owe little to phylogenetic heritage. Thus, it may be assumed that the modal personality of the high-pasturage ones is largely shaped by their ecology. This does not mean, however, that nothing of personality is transmitted as a part of the heritage which flows from the gene pools of the past to the populations of the present. As physical characteristics are known to pass from generation to generation, so it would seem that something of character—or the raw stuff of character in glandular balance or imbalance and functioning—is inherited.

Take, for example, the personality trait of bravery, the ideal of which, without doubt, is culturally transmitted. Yet bravery, in its manifestations, is often linked with hardihood, which, in turn, may owe much to inherited as well as developed physical endurance. Nor does everyone have the same degree of adrenal glandular reaction to danger and the variables of the endowment are, to some degree, a matter of heredity. The ancestors of the nomadic pastoralists were rebels, adventurers, and those who broke from the safe and sure into the taking of risks. Selective processes that are partly bioenvironmental and partly cultural have produced descendants who are hardy risk-takers.

Childhood Experiential Determinants

From birth the children of this society are subjected to contrasting stimuli. The newborn arriving, possibly, a few days before time because of the effects of altitude, or because his mother had to ride up to the very day of delivery, is most welcome and tenderly cared for, as children are much wanted. For the first few months the infant spends much of his time in comfort within the blouse of his mother's sheepskin coat, bare skin next to bare skin and with access to her breasts whenever he is hungry. But he is weaned much earlier than most Asian children, for his mother needs to be free for herd chores and milking, and that very milk is also available for substitute feeding. He even rides with her during that period, head sticking out of her coat like the head of a baby kangeroo. When not thus with his mother, he is kept in a sheltered nook within the tent, warmly tucked away among bits of sheepskin and felt.

By contrast he also knows stress from the time of his very first ride as the rhythms and uncertainties of movement ahorseback are communicated to him with startling abruptness within his mother's coat. Very soon after—his mother needing to be free to react to the exigencies of the trail—he finds himself packed in a bag or basket as one-half of an ox load and carried erratically by a wayward yak that will not stay on the trail. When he can hold on to someone's girdle he rides behind the saddle, clutching for dear life, and soon after that stage he is put on a saddle that has a frame in front on which to hold tight, and so he rides alone. In these moves, sheltered and wrapped though he may be, he yet knows, all alone, rain in his face and storm and discomfort while his parents are busied with necessary chores.

His association with animals has much of the same sharp contrast. When, rolling or crawling, he first begins to move within the tent, he comes into contact with the young of animals, puppies, lambs, or an occasional calf brought in for shelter. They are furry, warm, and good playmates, and playmates of his own kind are both scarce and hard to contact in the encampment. The grown dogs too are friendly, licking his face and sometimes helping to clean him when he has messed, but they are the ones of his own tent. With the first steps which take him outside of that tent he learns of those other, not so friendly, dogs; he learns too of danger, very real, and just beyond the limits of where his own furry friends make a zone of safety. The consciousness of danger comes early and haunts his childhood, changing, as he becomes an adult, into caution, linked, however, with ability to defend himself. Yet he has learned that menace is an inseparable part of life as it must be lived.

Play and contact with the young animals also leads into his first experimentation in the mastery of beasts, as he runs to separate the lambs from the ewes before milking, helps tether stock, and, a little later, holds the nose rope of an ox that is being loaded. The many chores of pastoralism and the chronic shortage of manpower that characterizes the economy push the child, boy or girl, very early toward assumption of adult roles.

Increasingly, he experiences success in controlling beasts larger than himself, and the pattern and expectation of mastery, with all its ego satisfactions and assurance of dominance, become a part of emerging personality. Half-child and half-adult, he early lays claim to recognition as one who can meet each challenge and perform like a high-pasturage one should.

Situational Determinants

General situational determinants such as environment, diet, and movement affect both children and adults. Specific situations such as subsistence exigencies, horsemanship, and risk-and-security factors affect children in proportion to the extent they progressively assume adult roles.

Environment engulfs everyone. There is no existence away from it and from the variables which have been described. Some of these environmental variables have, or are suspected of having, certain effects on psychological or emotional reaction. Altitude, which includes many unknowns such as increased irradiation (cosmic, ultraviolet, and the like) and changed blood pressure, appears to produce alternations of tension and lethargy, and levels of insomnia. Scarcity of oxygen produces physiological changes affecting body chemistry and function that affect personality; heightened sensitivity to drugs and alcohol, which, in their effects, are also conditioned by personality variables; and states of alternating euphoria and irritability. Seasonal temperature alternation has been tentatively correlated with increased energy output, and has been offered as one explanation for the temperate-zone richness in cultural achievement. The extreme diurnal changes in temperature on the Tibetan plateau, to which the body and personality must react, certainly is a continual stimulant.

The net result of these and other influences is a personality keyed to a high pitch and tightly strung. The immediacy and pace of activity within an encampment well exemplifies such personality in action. At altitudes where everyone is short of breath, tasks are done in an on-the-run pace that is needless and seems compulsive. That a herder, when controlling stock, rides at the fastest gait the terrain will permit is reasonable. That tasks such as catching and shearing sheep, tethering, or packing loads, which involve the handling of restive animals are done on-the-run is understandable. But to bale wool or take down a tent and fold it at the same, or simulated, pace, to the accompaniment of breathless puffing, like a swimmer doing a fast crawl, make activity seem like a compulsive race, in continuous competition with someone else, or with oneself.

Research on how diet may affect personality is so far mostly inconclusive, yet high-protein intake has been linked with high-energy output, and a sense of vigor, waiting to be paired with initiative, must have its effect on personality. In trade, the equal value, by weight, of meat and barley, and the daily menu of the pastoralists indicate an impressive intake of protein, with animal fats to complement its transformation into energy, assuring an ample high-protein source of energy.

Movement as a determinant may only be argued inferentially, for there are no data on how motion, as such, affects personality. Those, however, who most exemplify exposure to its influence—the caravaneers of the Middle East, the muleteers of Chinese roads, or the truckdrivers of the American highways—are all versions of one recognizable stereotype, closely resembling the nomadic pastoralists of Tibet. They are tough, self-reliant, meeting emergencies as mere routine, and subtly alert to changes of weather, scene, and circumstance; for the change that goes with movement is a variable requiring constant, focused attention.

Subsistence exigencies, and the multivariant responses they trigger, constitute the most comprehensive category of situational determinants. These exigencies consist of specific problems to be solved, challenges to be met, and emergencies to be overcome, or at least weathered. Some arise in the routines of pastoralism, others in the movements of nomadism. They are innumerable and of infinite variety, but a few typical instances may be cited: a grass fire threatens to burn the winter-quarters pasturage or, out of control, does destroy it; traders try to drive infected livestock (animals with rinderpest, or hoof-and-mouth disease, for example) through communal territory; scabies is discovered in the sheep herd; the horse herd is stampeded by a thunder storm and takes off at high speed; wolves are sighted or suspicious tracks of unknown horsemen are seen; straying stock get caught in bogs or quicksand; oxen spill tenthold belongings along the trail and scatter with pack ropes dragging; a rider's own mount gets dangerously trapped in deep snow or treacherous bog; the horse herd is driven off by raiders [see Ekvall (1954c:69–74) for a description of such a raid]; yak and *mDZo* cows sneak away to return to where they dropped last year's calves; the trail of the grain caravan is blocked by a sudden spread of glare ice from spring seepage; rivers too deep to ford must be crossed in the search for lost cattle; and so forth, in numberless permutations.

In all their variety, the responses which these and similar exigencies trigger have certain common denominators: realistic appraisal of just exactly what is happening in a photoflash recognition of relevancies; near-instantaneous making of decisions; *ad hoc* and all-out commitment, as suggested in the Tibetan words for decision making, *THag CHod* (cut-off rope); action swift as a reflex, but carried through to the end. Such a pattern of behavior, endlessly repeated into habit, must shape, or mark, the modal personality.

The high-pasturage ones also have, and ride, the horse, though it does not have the same place in the economy as among the typical horse-culture pastoralists (Mongol, Kirghiz, and the like). The Tibetan horse is a sturdy, pony-sized (12 to 14½-hands) animal of amazing toughness, which exhibits such variations in conformation, color, and gaits as might indicate multiple origins. Grays, from near-black to near-white, predominate, but blacks, sorrels, buckskins, roans, bays, and even apaloosa-marked animals are not uncommon. As legends

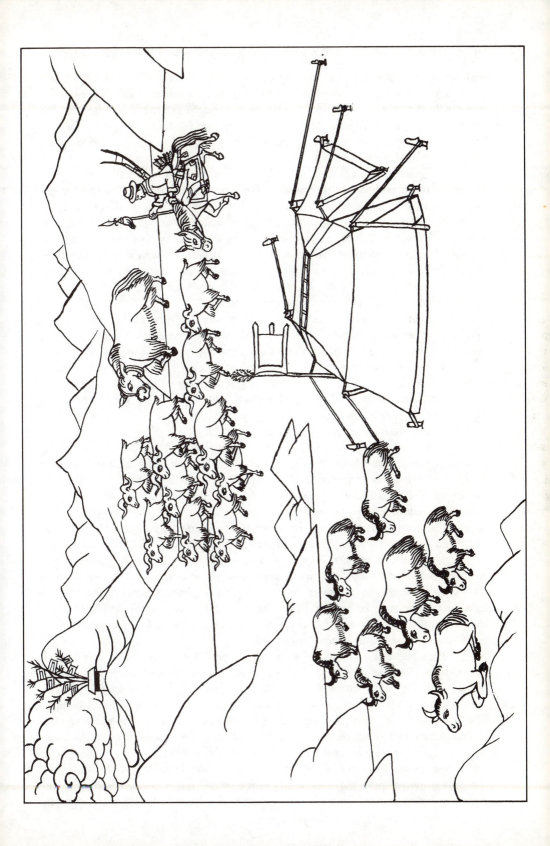

and the resemblance between two words for horse, Tibetan *rTa* and Ural-Altaic *agta*, suggest, the horse probably was an early import from northern horse-culture peoples; however, a very ancient Tibetan term *rMang* (mount) does resemble the Burmese word *rming* (horse), which also suggests that some of the early Tibetans, who possibly came from the south, shared knowledge, and use, of the small-boned hill pony of Southeast Asia.

The horse has a place in the culture of the nomadic pastoralists somewhat analogous to its position in the culture of the nomadic pastoralists of Arabia. In both cultures it is linked with raiding and the making of war. Is never eaten, as among the horse-culture peoples, and is a status symbol of great emotional account. Like the Arabs, the Tibetans take the best care they can of their horses, making sure they are well blanketed, even if the rider sleeps less warmly; sharing food with them to the extent that I have seen horses eating, with seeming relish, shavings of dried meat; and developing a repertoire of legends and songs concerning the exploits, qualities, and appearance of their steeds.

The breaking in of the horse, done mostly by very young men, is the apotheosis of the mastering of beasts that marks the experience of the child through youthhood to manhood. It is done in stages. First the colt is bit-broken by having ropes attached to both rings of the snaffle bit and being pulled from side to side, and to a halt, until it responds readily. Then it is mounted and ridden bareback. Only after it has ceased to fight the bareback rider is it ridden with a saddle, a high-treed frame with very short stirrup leathers which put the rider into a "crouch" seat, somewhat like an exaggerated "Italian" or "jump" seat.

What riding does to the rider is hard to evaluate. "The man on horseback" is not a figure of speech so much as a reflection of historical and psychological truth. It is realization of the myth of the centaur in which the purpose and intelligence of the man is merged with the fleetness and strength of the horse to become something beyond the human in a sense of power and a reflection of pride.

The reality of that pride is embedded in many languages: The Chinese ideograph for pride is a combination of the symbols of ride, high, and horse; and in raucous argument we say, "Come off your high horse." In funeral ceremonies, too, the final sad humbling of pride is signalized by the riderless horse that follows on the last journey. To whatever degree the Tibetan nomadic pastoralist, by the habit of riding and the feel of power between his knees, is touched with such megalomania of power and pride intertwined, then riding, as an experience in itself, plays a part in shaping personality.

That possession of the horse, and the special mobility which it provides for both evasion and attack, predisposes a community to the making of war is self-evident. The affect introduction of the horse had on Plains Indians is a well-known example of the changes which follow the impact of the horse on a culture. The association of weaponry with being ahorseback is well celebrated in the legends, epics, and songs of the high-pasturage ones. The one riding the excellent horse, to guard the herds, is the one with threefold armament—sword, arrow (or gun), and spear. That this combination, in ideal and in actuality, should foster warmaking propensities and acts of aggression is also self-evident. The case of the PHu Ma Kyang I Hang nomads of south-central Tibet brings some evidence in reverse to this question of the relationship between horsemanship and weaponry and the disposition to make war. They are "true" nomads, having no link with any community, yet they insist they are not like other nomads for they have little strife amongst themselves and none with other communities—they are at peace. However, unlike other nomads, they have no horses, or tradition of horsemanship, and the men do not wear swords, only stubby half-swords which are used in cutting the sod with which they make their shelters.

This aspect of horsemanship, as a personality determinant, leads directly into the problem of risk and security in the same determinant role. The consciousness of danger as one of the facts of life that begins so early in the experience of the pastoralist child is not lost as the man learns to take care and fend off the dogs, but grows into wary acceptance of danger, most of it from human greed, truculence, and enmity, as a basic dimension of existence.

It is fear of the greed of others which sets a man at watch on the rim of the encampment with his weapons in bed with him, that causes the herdsmen to make his noon campfires on hilltops so that he can watch on all sides and keep the herds in full view, and that makes him suspect every lone unidentified rider of being a thief. It is his own, and his fellow's truculence that puts his hand so frequently on the handle of his sword, which may be drawn as deftly as the "fast draw" in a "western movie," when a dispute becomes a quarrel. The greatest number of wounds which I treated as an amateur doctor were sword wounds, and a noticeable number of grown men carried scars. It is enmity, however, which imposes the greatest degree of wary caution and a tense, coiled-spring readiness for counteraction. Every unresolved quarrel, every seduction and elopement, every raid, and every blood feud—most serious of all, with its bitter claims to vengeance— is a source of enmity to be feared. Men sleep, when bivouacking, in the shadows away from the fire so the glow will not make them targets; ride wearisome patrols to forestall surprise attack; approach mountain passes by making traverses, when possible, on slopes overlooking places where trails notch the crest, to avoid being ambushed; and, if it can be done, ride always with at least one companion.

This ever-present menace—the risk against which security must be maintained—makes the high-pasturage ones suspicious and wary, but also aggressively ready for violent response. Another kind of risk, moreover, is inherent in the economy of the pastoralists, and has its own particular affect on modal personality. The economy is a high-risk one with very little of the slow-but-sure aspect of gain, for the livestock fields of the agriculturalists are as vulnerable as the harvests. A single heavy snowstorm, or a virulent cattle epidemic, can virtually wipe out all the potential harvest *and* the fields as well, leaving the once wealthy pastoralist a pauper. Loss and gain are equally unpredictable, for in two or three very good seasons a poor man can become a man of wealth, but risk is always present.

With acceptance of risk as the basic factor, the subsistence routine becomes a successive taking of chances, and when risk taking becomes a habit, the habit may well leave its mark on personality, thus giving to the nomadic pastoralist something of the character and outlook of the gambler. This may partially explain his lavishness, his love of status symbols, and his arrogant assurance in situations of disaster, for chance, that has gone against him, may well be with him next time.

Ethos-Cultural Determinants

The ethos of a culture, sometimes defined as its *spirit*, is a strangely elusive concept. The search for it may be the painstaking effort to distill an essence from observed behavior patterns, personality data, and even such material as the character-trait lists in this text; or it may be a kind of detective work in which clues, found in the most unexpected places, may be of significance.

In the tradition of culture-and-language theory two items of linguistic usage—one the turn of a phrase and one the content of a epithet or compliment— seem to express ethos ideals and relate to modal personality. These ideals may either be *characterizations* of the personality, or, by evoking conformity, be *determinants*.

There is a common greeting, in the form of a question, to which I have never heard an affirmative answer. *E dKaa THal?* ("Has there been difficulty?") is the question which is asked of the guest as he enters the tent, is shouted to riders coming within earshot from every form of venture, trade, hunting, raiding, pilgrimage, or long-range herding, and is posed to the members of the tenthold as they gather at the end of the day's activities. The invariable answer is *Ma dKaa THal* (There has been no difficulty), or, more colloquially, "No trouble at all," like a flippant brush-off of an unwarranted aspersion.

The hard fact is, that, in every instance, there has been plenty of trouble. No day filled with the exigencies of pastoralism combined with nomadism can be without trouble. Repeatedly, I have traveled with Tibetans when the entire day has been a succession of disasters or near-disasters: loads thrown in bogs and streams; robbers evaded or, in head-on confrontation, bluffed off; rain all day, so hard that no noon halt was feasible and everyone went hungry and thirsty; what should have been fords become waters for swimming, with loads and cattle nearly swept away; and at the end we were a sorry bedraggled lot, but the answer, somewhat hoarsely defiant and denying all reality, remained true to form—*Ma dKaa THal* (No difficulty at all).

This—what the French call a *qualité*—is hardly a "world view" or even a "dominant value," but, if language has any metalinguistic significance, here is something which is a part of ethos to function as a determinant of modal personality. It enunciates an ideal—utter denial of difficulty—and insists there can be no weakening.

The boasting of the high-pasturage ones has been mentioned, but the self-image projected by a compliment in common use is authentic beyond any calculated formulation, as unconsciously revealing as the words by which men swear, and invoked with equal frequency. *Bu rGod* (son untamed), warm with the affection of family, but often part of an encouraging war cry, concisely sums up the ideal man. In a Tibetan-Tibetan dictionary *rGod* is defined as "not subdued" and "like high pasturage not domesticated." "Son untamed" is the criterion by which men are judged to be able, dependable, undaunted, and fit to play any role— even the ultimate one when life and death are at issue. *AH Bu rGod KHyod* (Hail sons untamed you) is the universal compliment, the acknowledgment one offers, in good fellowship and admiration, to praise achievement, or in simple flattery. *Bu rGod Ma* (son untamed female) also is the best way to thank a tentwife for a bowl of yoghurt, and in response she probably will give you a second helping along with the warmest of smiles.

The term probably says most aptly what the culture hero should be. There is another definitive word for hero, having an important place in mythology, history, and even mysticism, but it is seldom invoked. Rather, the high-pasturage ones prefer to be known as untamed.

The word *rGod* as verb also means "to laugh," and though psychologists say that laughter is aggressive in nature, the connection between laughter and "untamed" is, perhaps, a mockingly mysterious part of the ethos of this culture. At any rate, there is a beguiling lack of grimness, and frequent, boisterous, laughter among the "untamed sons" of the high pasturage.

Survival or Change after the Chinese Take-Over

S URVIVAL OR CHANGE for these people and their culture, in the normal course of events, would be a step-by-step integration within a changing national economy, and steady movement—sometimes hastened by traumatic impact—toward modernization. It would then be just another case history of how a nomadic pastoralist society comes to terms with the facts of the modern world, not too different from what is taking place in Iran, North Africa, and even Mongolia.

The communist Chinese take-over of Tibet—which began in 1950, reached a climax in 1959, and is still not entirely completed—lifted the problem to a different level of significance. Survival or change for the nomadic pastoralists became not just a question of their own fate but a test whether or not they might be able to save significant portions of the culture of Tibet from destruction or a sad, changed-beyond-recognition state.

Knowing the high-pasturage ones, it is now necessary to learn something of Chinese policy and its implementation in order to evaluate the chance of survival or project a pattern of change. Communist Chinese policy with regard to the high-pasturage people, formulated in the mystique of communism according to Mao, had a basis of both knowledge and need.

Knowledge Basis of Chinese Policy

In the framework of communist doctrine and experience—particularly in Russian experience with their own nomadic pastoralists in central Asia—there is no logical and acceptable place for the nomad. He and his economy do not fit into Marxist theory of the socialist state, and the Russians found it expedient to eradicate nomadic pastoralism as a system. Thus, when the Chinese turned their attention to the unfinished business of Tibet, they were impelled to make an end of the nomads once and for all.

There was, however, another framework of experiential knowledge that also affected policy making. The leaders, from Mao Tse-tung on down, had bitter, first-hand knowledge of the harsh ecology of the high pasturage, of the rich resources but evasive quality of its economy, and of the unfriendly truculence of its inhabitants. The justly famed Long March (1935–1936) did have its nonsuccesses and, near its end, the attempt by the Chinese to cross the northeastern corner of the Tibetan plateau was a disaster.

Ten years later the communist Chinese leaders whom I met in Peking still shivered and shuddered when they talked about the high grassland and the elusive, unfriendly, people who lived there, whom they could neither convert nor defeat. Veterans who—fighting by day and marching by night—had made their way across half of China could not even come to grips with the horsemen who sniped at them and vanished. Those swift riders did not need to close in for the kill. They knew that cold, hunger, and heart strain, from the exertion of trying to match horsemen in mobility at high altitude, would take their toll as the Chinese died by the many thousands.

Need Basis of Chinese Policy

The realities of Chinese need—often at odds with theory—also affected policy making. The protein-hungry Chinese people needed the beeves and muttons of the high pasturage and the industries of China needed the wool, hides, salt, and borax that the pastoralists produced. Nor could the Chinese substitute their own manpower as they can do so easily in agricultural production. Under the most favorable conditions they are not, except in keeping pigs and ducks, a livestock people, and it takes long acclimatization, extending, possibly, through more than one life cycle, to fit people to operate energetically and successfully at 16,000 feet above sea level. The Chinese needed to have effective control of the pastoralists, who themselves controlled the resources, exploitation, and transportation of the plateau.

Policy and Its Implementation

Chinese policy with regard to how the high-pasturage ones and their economy were to be incorporated into the socialist state, and the implementation of that policy, exhibited strange hesitations and vacillations, reflecting the dilemma inherent in the contradictions between theory, realistic knowledge of conditions, and pressing needs.

At the beginning the Chinese temporized. The policy was, in effect, to leave the pastoralists alone. While land reform and the first steps toward collectivization were being pushed elsewhere, the pastoralists were told there would be no such change for them. They were to carry on pastoralism as they always had and keep producing livestock and wool, for which they would get good prices. They were assured that socialization was years away and then only when they wished it. The compulsions of ideology, however, soon moved the Chinese to take the first steps toward socialization according to Mao and tentatively introduce collectivization. From the experience of the Chinese peasantry there were two tried and outstandingly successful preliminary steps to be taken. By agitation and propaganda they could (a) set the "have nots" against the "haves," and (b) engineer redistribution of land by community action through "peoples' courts."

Such tactics did not produce the anticipated results for a number of reasons. In the relative affluence of the pastoralist society the true have nots were none too numerous. Even when found, they had much more than some sharecropping Chinese peasant had ever had and, though relatively poor, each one continued to sense the opportunity inherent in pastoralism and, with the gambler's outlook, could always hope for better luck next season. Redistribution of land, all aspects of which were most familiar to the Chinese, meant nothing as an issue, for the land already was communally owned and redistribution of fields on the hoof was strangely new, complicated, and quite outside Chinese experience. The measurements of soil fields, and primary ownership, were fixed and known. But livestock fields shift in size, and primary ownership fluctuates in ways that are not within the pattern underlying the Chinese agrarian revolution. Furthermore, ownership is a peculiarly personal relationship which made separating a man from his animals, and from his personalized care of them, a delicate matter.

However tentative such steps were, they were resented as attempts to disrupt the society and the economy. From the first stirrings of unease, situations such as these develop in a classic pattern. Pressure is followed by resentment, coercion by nonconformity, the use of force by rebellion, reprisal by counterviolence on an ever increasing scale, and, in the end, war. At each stage in this fateful chain of action and events the Chinese were to find that their initial foreknowledge of difficulty and caution was well-founded; the reaction of the high-pasturage ones was more violent than expected; their nomadic ability to save themselves, their dwellings, and their fields—in effect to "get out from under the blow"—made reprisal discouragingly ineffective; and, when they finally went to war, their temperament, equipment, and trained capability in the techniques of warfare on the Tibetan plateau made them formidable opponents.

This linkage of action and reaction, inevitable though it might be, was not uniformly continuous nor the same in all localities. There were many starts and stops and erratic synchronization. At one time all pressure was lifted and the Chinese cadres were, in their turn—and to their bewilderment, no doubt—sternly lectured on: the necessity of having a nondoctrinaire approach to their work; being willing to take counsel with the herdsmen and listen to them; developing a "work style" that was adapted to the actual conditions; avoiding an attitude of intolerance and anything that resembled "great-Han chauvinism"; carefully doing nothing that would hamper full development of the resources of the grasslands. Apparently, production of livestock, wool, hides, and the like, to meet Chinese requirements, had suffered.

During one of these pauses in implementation a three-point project was launched with the slogan (there always must be a slogan) "fixed abodes and nomadic herding." It was stressed that fixed abode, affording some comfort and optimum protection against the rigors of the climate, provided the best conditions for the development of the individual and the society. But it was also conceded that full exploitation of the plateau required the movement of herds throughout the high pasturage.

To achieve these goals a program was outlined that was mostly carrot with scarcely any stick showing. The Chinese would set up, in sheltered lower areas, veterinarian service stations where the herdsmen could have their stock inoculated against epidemic diseases and receive treatment for other disorders. At, or near, these stations it was proposed to build and staff schools where the children could be educated—and also indoctrinated—for their roles in the new Tibet. The third and most important part of the program had to do with supplementary feed—hay, turnips, or grain crops (oats, for example), cut green and dried for fodder— during the "starvation time" of winter. This is a very real and pressing need, and to meet the need, plans were outlined to help the Tibetans to open up fodder-crop fields; build shelters in which to store such crops; put up shelter sheds for stock; build huts where the sick, aged, and those who could be spared from actual herding operations could stay; and, by combining the manpower this made available with the ready supply of animal products, establish small-scale industries.

All these proposals answered real needs and unquestionably offered some attractive inducements, but the real objective is obvious: to tie the nomadic pastoralist to a fixed locale, by anchoring permanently some part of his family, wealth, or concerns. Then, wherever he wanders in "nomadic herding," he must return to that point and has lost something of mobility and the freedom that goes with it; becoming more easily controlled.

Together with such enticements the nomadic pastoralists still receive preferential treatment—whenever they are not involved in outright confrontation. As late as 1963, when all of Tibetan agriculture had been fully collectivized, the nomads were still being allowed private ownership of all their stock, and were being told that, if they would just keep producing animal products in ever increasing quantities, they were under no pressure to accept immediate socialization of their economy.

How they respond to enticement, preferential treatment, and the ultimate pressures that will be brought to bear upon them is the key to their survival, but the Chinese need gives them—temporarily, at least—a chance to remain the pastoralists of the Tibetan plateau for some time. They are certain to resist change, to the best of their not inconsiderable powers of noncompliance and evasion, but their nomadism will slowly and surely become compromised as they learn to operate under the slogan "fixed habitation and nomadic herding."

As heritors of Tibetan culture, because of their conservatism and their self-image, they will retain, with minimal distortion, the essentials of Tibetan culture for a longer period than elsewhere. They may not be, as once assumed, the original Tibetans, but they see themselves as the most Tibetan of all Tibetans, what Professor Stein (1963:97) calls *les vrais Tibetains, et les plus purs*; and, as the untamed sons of the high pasturage, consciously or unconsciously, dedicated to the role of making the last stand.

References

CUTTING, SUYDAM, 1940, *The Fire Ox and Other Years.* New York: Charles Scribner's Sons.

DOWNS, JAMES F., 1964, "Livestock, Production, and Social Mobility in High Altitude Tibet," *American Anthropologist,* Vol. 66, pp. 1115–1119.

———— and ROBERT B. EKVALL, 1965, "Animal and Social Types in the Exploitation of the Tibetan Plateau," in *Man, Culture and Animals,* eds. Anthony Leeds and Andrew P. Vayda. Washington-American Association for the Advancement of Science.

EDGERTON, ROBERT B., 1965, " 'Cultural' vs. 'Ecological' Factors in the Expression of Values, Attitudes, and Personality Characteristics," *American Anthropologist,* Vol. 67, pp. 442–447.

EKVALL, ROBERT B., 1939, *Cultural Relations on the Kansu-Tibetan Border.* Chicago: University of Chicago Press.

————, 1952, *Tibetan Skylines.* New York: Farrar, Straus & Giroux, Inc.

————, 1954a, "Some Differences in Tibetan Land Tenure and Utilization," *Sinologica,* Vol. 1, pp. 39–48.

————, 1954b, *"Mi sTong:* The Tibetan Custom of Life Indemnity," *Sociologus,* Vol. 2, pp. 136–145.

————, 1954c, *Tents against the Sky.* London: Victor Gollancz, Ltd.

————, 1961c, "The Nomadic Pattern of Living among the Tibetans as Preparation for War," *American Anthropologist,* Vol. 63, pp. 1250–1263.

————, 1963a, "Some Aspects of Divination in Tibetan Society," *Ethnology,* Vol. 1, pp. 31–39.

————, 1964b, "Peace and War among the Tibetan Nomads," *American Anthropologist,* Vol. 66, pp. 1119–1148.

————, 1964c, *Religious Observances in Tibet: Patterns and Function.* Chicago: The University of Chicago Press.

FEILBERG, C. G., 1944, *La Tente Noire.* Copenhagen: I Kommission hos Gyldendal.

GOLDSCHMIDT, WALTER, 1964, "Theory and Strategy in the Study of Cultural Adaptability," *American Anthropologist,* Vol. 67, pp. 402–408.

KRADER, LAWRENCE, 1959, "The Ecology of Nomadic Pastoralism," *International Social Science Journal,* pp. 499–510.

STEIN, R. A., 1962, *La Civilisation Tibetaine.* Paris: Dunod.

Recommended Reading List

The following three books treat exclusively of Tibetan nomadic pastoralism:

HERMANNS, MATHIAS, 1949, *Die Nomaden von Tibet*. Vienna: Verlag Herold.
> A book in which first-hand personal observation of some nomadic pastoralists in the extreme northeastern tip of ethnic Tibet is combined with considerable analysis and theorizing along lines of the Vienna school of ethnology. Has much real substance.

EKVALL, ROBERT B., 1952, *Tibetan Skylines*. New York: Farrar, Straus & Giroux, Inc.; London: Victor Gollancz, Ltd.
> A collection of personality vignettes and descriptions of happenings in nomadic pastoral communities of northeast Tibet. Acceptably authentic and true to life.

———, 1954, *Tents against the Sky*. New York: Farrar, Straus & Giroux, Inc.; London: Victor Gollancz, Ltd.
> A novel, with setting and characters among Tibetan pastoralists, which was characterized in a New York *Times* book review as "of indifferent quality as fiction but most excellent ethnography."

The following books describe different but representative nomadic pastoral societies:

BARTH, FREDRIK, 1961, *Nomads of South-Persia*. New York: Humanities Press, Inc.
> Detailed and comprehensive description of a nomadic society whose pastoralism is based principally on sheep. Of special interest are the complicated patterns of seasonal migration, some indication of transference of interest from pastoralism to agriculturalism, and the marked mobility of the family.

BRIGGS, LLOYD CABOT, 1960, *Tribes of the Sahara*. Cambridge: Harvard University Press.
> This survey is comprehensive and detailed. Patterns of relationship with agricultural communities, the importance of trade, and the tradition of raiding are of special interest. Contrasts with, and similarities to, Tibetan nomadic pastoralism are noteworthy.

KRADER, LAWRENCE, 1963, *Social Organization of the Mongol-Turkic Pastoral Nomads*. The Hague: Mouton.
> Emphasis is on social structure—principally the family—to the exclusion of much

else, but in the preliminary and final portions of each section devoted to a particular people there is some treatment of the more general aspects of central Asian nomadic pastoralism and discussion of how nomadism has been reduced under Soviet control.

LATTIMORE, OWEN, 1962, *Nomads and Commissars*. New York: Oxford University Press.

An authoritative discussion of contemporary pastoralism in Mongolia as observed in 1961. The maintenance of pastoralism through the modification of traditional patterns, coupled with the reduction of nomadizing and a limited shift toward agriculture, are of particular interest.

UNESCO, 1959, "Nomads and Nomadism in the Arid Zone," *International Social Science Journal*, Vol. 11, No. 4.

This collection of nine papers by various experts in the field is a most valuable survey of arid-zone nomadic pastoralism. Not only is the material most varied, taken from across north Africa through to the heart of Asia, but it is treated from a variety of viewpoints, including the Russian.